Sexual Abuse
PREVENTION

A Course of Study for Teenagers

Revised and Updated

Rebecca Voelkel-Haugen
and Marie M. Fortune

UNITED CHURCH PRESS
Cleveland, Ohio

United Church Press, Cleveland, Ohio 44115
© 1996 by United Church Press

Biblical quotations are from the New Revised Standard Version of the Bible,
© 1989 by the Division of Christian Education of the National Council of the Churches of Christ in the U.S.A.,
and are used by permission

Printed in the United States of America on acid-free paper
01 00 99 98 97 96   5 4 3 2 1

Voelkel-Haugen, Rebecca.
    Sexual abuse prevention : a course of study for teenagers /
Rebecca Voelkel-Haugen and Marie M. Fortune.
      p.   cm.
    Rev. and updated ed. of: Sexual abuse prevention, c1984.
    ISBN 0-8298-1082-X (alk. paper)
    1. Child sexual abuse—Prevention—Study and teaching—
United States. 2. Rape—Prevention—Study and teaching—United
States. I. Fortune, Marie M. II. Fortune, Marie M. Sexual abuse
prevention. III. Title.
HQ72.U53B63 1996
362.7'68—dc20   96-458
                                                       CIP

*To all the young women and men who have survived sexual abuse
and live each day with tremendous courage, faith, and hope.
And to the women and men, especially those at the Center for the
Prevention of Sexual and Domestic Violence, who witness to the truth
that the way things are is not the way they have to be.*

Contents

Foreword

The first edition of this book was published in 1984. Life even then was simpler for adolescents than it is now nearer the end of the twentieth century. The statistics tell us why: one in three females (Diana Russell) and one in seven males (David Finkelhor) is sexually abused before the age of eighteen, usually by a family member or close friend. These figures also apply to the young people in our church youth groups—in every youth group there are both female and male survivors of childhood sexual abuse.

According to Washington, D.C., researchers Debra Boyer and David Fine, authors of a detailed 1992 study of young women who became pregnant during adolescence, a significant number have been physically or sexually abused at home. Boyer and Fine found that of the young women they interviewed, two-thirds had been raped or sexually abused, nearly always by fathers, stepfathers, or other relatives or guardians. Other studies also show that the younger the girl who has engaged in sexual intercourse, the more likely that the sexual encounter was not consensual, and the more likely that the encounter was with an adult male.[1]

Interestingly, preadolescent girls avoid a lot of male peer harassment because they spend most of their time with other girls. Hence these girls are more self-assured, outspoken, in charge of themselves (Carol Gilligan). However, with adolescence comes vulnerability to male abuse for three reasons: (1) females are taught that their value depends on attracting men; thus heterosexual young women feel less than okay when not in a relationship with a male; (2) young men are learning simultaneously that they are in a privileged position vis-à-vis young women, a position they can maintain by force if necessary, without consequences; (3) as young women's sexual development becomes apparent, young men relate to them primarily as sex objects.[2]

Researchers have found that the increased psychological trauma experienced by adolescent girls corresponds to the increased time they spend in cross-sex interaction (Maccoby, 1990). It appears that the development of male identity occurs at the expense of females' safety. As one young woman put it, in the process of becoming adolescents "our lives [get] smaller and smaller, our days [get] shorter and shorter" (Herbert, 1989: 84).[3]

For males, the trauma of peer harassment usually takes the form of verbal or physical abuse directed at any male who is perceived as "different." As I stood in a checkout line listening to two mothers discuss their sons, one asked the other if her son was playing football this season. The other mother said, "Yes, he is, but he doesn't really want to."

"Then why is he?" asked the first mother.

"Because he doesn't want to be called a sissy," replied the second.

Whether the motivating factor is homophobia and the aggression directed at boys who are thought to be gay ("queer bashing") or is merely abuse directed at the younger, smaller, nonathletic boys who actually prefer to treat girls with respect, it is not easy for males who don't buy the "real man" model to get through adolescence unscathed.

Add to this a media context in which music, film, computer resources, and advertising blatantly diminish and humiliate women and glorify male control of "their" women, often with overt violent images. Whatever the source, it requires enormous energy to shield oneself from the relentless onslaught of verbal abuse, unwanted touch, and overt assault.

In this article from a Melbourne, Australia, newspaper, Rachael Horsfield describes her experience:

"Blondes have more fun." I wonder what the sense is behind this statement, because I find it awfully ironic as I reflect on what I am subjected to each day as I walk to and from school.

I am 16 years old. I have long blonde hair and am tall. I have begun to regard my appearance as a disadvantage because of the fear and discomfort I have experienced. I have suddenly realized that I fit a female stereotype set by men. So, to me, the claim that "blondes have more fun" is a patriarchal myth. . . .

Take today, for example. In the walk to and from my friend's place in the middle of the day, I encountered at least five separate incidents of men whistling, yelling "pet" names and making vulgar, degrading motions and signs towards me. The funny thing is that, until recently, it never hit me just how frequently this occurs. . . .

Not only do I not like it, but it scares me. . . . All this happens in busy streets in front of people who stand there looking at me as if I were to blame. They don't look at the cause of the noise and abuse, they stare at me. Not once have I had someone stick up for me. . . .

I have the right to feel safe anywhere. Why should 16-year-old girls have to put up with this?[4]

This is the common experience of teenage girls (and some boys). The harassment may come from strangers on the street, or from peers as they walk down the hall at school, or as they engage in an intimate relationship. When I was meeting with parents of youth group members in a local church a number of years ago, introducing them to the sexual abuse prevention curriculum for their sons and daughters, one father raised his hand to ask a question: "All I want to know is, are you going to tell them what is right and what is wrong?" I hesitated, knowing that he was looking for the abstinence speech, and then replied, "Yes, I will tell them that it is wrong to coerce or force anyone to do something sexual and it is right to share sexual activity in a context of respect, commitment, and equality." He looked puzzled. I knew that I had not satisfied him, but at least I gave him something to think about.

These two experiences, one from the perspective of a young woman and the other from the perspective of a parent of a young woman, illustrate the glaring contradiction between teens' experiences and the context of adult (and usually church) responses.

What do these studies and stories tell us about the day-to-day stress of being an adolescent, of trying to survive growing up with any sense of self? And what are our churches doing about it?

Our task as the church is twofold: first is to pay attention and find ways to respond to the very real experiences of incest, rape, molestation, and harassment that our young people, female and male, may well have experienced either as children or as teens. We have a pastoral responsibility to open our ears, eyes, and hearts by making a space in which youth can learn about abuse and disclose if they so choose. If they do disclose, we must be prepared to use all of our resources and to report to the appropriate authorities in order to protect these young persons from further harm. In addition, we have a moral responsibility to do everything we can to ensure that the adults who provide leadership in youth ministry do not violate the teens' boundaries, sexualize their relationship with them, or abuse them. When young people come to church, they should find a safe place, a place of respite from their home, school, or community in which they may be experiencing abuse or harassment.

Our second task is equally important. If a significant number of our youth find their first sexual experience to be a coercive one, how do we help educate them about sexuality? If the first sexual experience is coercive, it is easy to conclude (in the absence of any other data) that sex is something done *to* you, that you have no right to bodily integrity, that you have no real choice in this matter. Under these circumstances, it is difficult to develop a healthy sense of one's self as a sexual being, not to mention healthy relationships. Good sexuality education is imperative.[5]

This curriculum does not provide sexuality education. Nor should it be used *instead* of a good sexuality education program. But it does point up the need for providing a good sexuality program that reaches beyond a "just say no" abstinence program to help young people grapple with difficult and complex situations that they face. "Just say no" abstinence makes no sense if the majority of young women (under fourteen years) are dealing with situations of coercion.

So this curriculum attempts to address the experiences of date rape, stranger rape, and incestuous abuse and looks at the cultural context in which these experiences occur, with a special emphasis on the media, the source of much information and subsequent confusion about sexuality.

We cannot pretend to protect our young people from harm by shutting them away from the world and one other. We can protect them best with information and openness, with the encouragement of a critical mind and lessons in self-respect and self-esteem. This is the best vaccine we can use to inoculate them as they move about their world today.

Consider using this curriculum with the youth in your church as your gift to them. Someday they will thank you for it.

Marie M. Fortune

Preface

I come to this work for many reasons. But two of the most important ones are that I am a Christian and I am a survivor of adolescent date rape. The latter happened when I was fifteen years old.

It was my first date. When I got home, I didn't tell anyone, not my parents, not my friends, not my teachers, no one. The next morning I went to church. I sat through the service with a growing weight on my heart. I thought this was no place to talk about what had happened to me. The next day I went to school and the weight on my heart grew heavier. By Friday it was almost unbearable so I tried to tell a friend. Her reaction was that I was too intense and that she didn't want to be my friend anymore. With her words, I buried my pain deep within.

It wasn't until four years later that someone at the college I attended lectured in our dorm about sexual assault and abuse. It was the first time I had heard anyone talk about the issue. After she finished, I went up to her and told her what had happened to me. Because she had broken the taboo about talking about sexual abuse, I could break my silence.

It took another two years before I spoke of my experience in church. Thankfully, I was heard, supported, and encouraged to continue the healing process. Because of the meaning of my faith and the authority the church community has in my life, this acceptance allowed me to move to a place in the healing journey that I had previously been unable to reach.

As I've spoken and written about my rape, I've found that my experience is not uncommon. Often survivors keep silent for years. (One woman I talked with recently didn't speak of her childhood sexual abuse until she was sixty-four.) They fear what others will say, that people will blame them. They also fear what the church will say. It's often easier to keep silent in church than face the possibility that the religious community will say they deserved what they got.

But the experience of being violated sexually throws a person into crisis. It causes pain and suffering and often raises theological questions about God, evil, etc. How could God let this happen to me? Is God powerless against evil? Was this punishment for something I've done? Survivors ask these questions. And these questions can and should be talked about in church.

We also need to talk about why abuse happens in the first place. When one person violates another, the church has a responsibility to teach that this is wrong. Our call is to be a community that proclaims justice and right relationship.

And so, I come to the writing of this curriculum with the prayer that religious communities, in this case the Christian community, strive to be places where justice is taught and preached and where survivors of sexual abuse are invited to share their pain, speak their truths, and experience real healing.

Rebecca Voelkel-Haugen

Acknowledgments

A professor once told me that the most important part of any book was the acknowledgments. Her reasoning was that it is here that the reader begins to glimpse the love, support, insight, and hard work that extend far beyond any single author or authors. The reader begins to see the community and context out of which a work has grown.

I didn't fully grasp the significance of my professor's words until I started this project. This is, indeed, a community effort that has grown out of much conversation and shared wisdom. I am deeply indebted to all the people mentioned here and many more. For their careful review of the manuscript in draft form: Beth Basham, Mitzi Eilts, Anne Ellestad, Joan and John Gerlach, Judy and Darryl Haugen, and Eleta K. Wright.

Many of the books, videos, and other materials listed in the resource section were brought to my attention by friends and fellow survivors. In particular, Susan Kilheffer, librarian for Planned Parenthood of Connecticut, and Carolyn Hardin Engelhardt, of the Vieth Center at Yale Divinity School, were very helpful in directing me to useful resources. Laura Wood got me connected with the New England College Sexual Assault Network. For this important information, I am grateful.

This is a revision of Rev. Marie Fortune's 1984 publication of the same name. Her input and guidance have been crucial. Working with her on this project has, as any interaction with her does, taught me much. Marie is my teacher and mentor, and it is an honor to have been a colleague in revising her work.

We both want to thank Rachael Horsfield of Melbourne, Australia, for her courage and willingness to share her story, and for the opportunity to include some of it in the foreword.

Shana Denise Hormann, MSW, needs to be mentioned. It was out of her concern that abuse prevention efforts address the particular needs of teenagers that the first publication of *Sexual Abuse Prevention: A Study for Teenagers* grew.

Starting in the summer of 1991, the women of the Center for the Prevention of Sexual and Domestic Violence allowed me to participate in the very important work that they do. Their insight, support, and humor continue to be guiding wisdom for me. I especially want to thank Sandra Barone for coordinating the review process of this manuscript.

Kim Sadler, always an encouraging and friendly tone in her voice, served as editor for this work with United Church Press.

And finally, I want to thank Kris Voelkel-Haugen, without whom much of the work here would have been impossible. For words of support as I dreaded returning to the computer, for many delicious meals, and for constant and continual love, thank you.

As with any work, I as author take full responsibility for the final product. As I have worked, I have sought to listen, reflect, and pray. I hope that I have acted faithfully and that this might be one more piece in our collective work toward ending sexual abuse.

Rebecca Voelkel-Haugen

Purpose of This Course

WHY AN EDUCATION PROGRAM?

When confronting the deepening problems that adolescents have to face, the question of what to do arises. Especially with the question of sexual abuse, many have given up hope. However, in study after study, it is clear that education can make a difference.

This curriculum is designed to begin the process of talking with teenagers about sexual abuse in the belief that effective education is a key to effective prevention of sexual abuse/violence of children and adolescents. It will also help those who have already been victimized by breaking the silence surrounding sexual abuse/violence and giving victims/survivors a place and people with whom to continue the process of healing.

WHY A COURSE IN CHURCH?

The task of educating young people about sexual abuse is often left to the schools or, worse yet, left undone. Although some denominations are working to address these problems, local churches have, in large part, not taken responsibility in this project. But educating about sexual abuse is exactly what the church should be doing because it's about teaching values. Sexual abuse prevention begins with helping people value respect, equality, honesty, mutuality, and justice. And each of these is, at its core, a biblical and theological issue. Thus, the church is the perfect setting in which to raise the issue.

WHAT THIS COURSE IS NOT

It is important to say that this course is *not* a course about sexuality. However, it relies on solid sexuality education being taught to children and adolescents. It also does not cover information about HIV/AIDS or HIV/AIDS prevention. (For this the authors recommend *Affirming Persons—Saving Lives: AIDS Awareness and Prevention Education for Christian Education Settings*, a curriculum that addresses AIDS and AIDS-related concerns in candid and age-appropriate language; it is available through United Church Press.) This curriculum is one piece in the educational framework about healthy relationships and relationships that harm. The authors highly recommend that sexuality education, including HIV/AIDS information, be a part of the church school curriculum as well. In fact, as people were asked to review the manuscript for this curriculum, person after person has stressed this point. Teenagers need accurate, clear, and truthful information about sexuality if they are to make good choices between healthy and harmful relationships. Many denominations have curricula available. Contact your denominational offices for more information.

WHAT THIS COURSE IS

This course *is* an introduction to sexual abuse and harassment. It is designed to help participants distinguish healthy sexuality from sexual abuse/violence. The ability to distinguish the two begins with understanding the dynamics at work in abuse. And so, this curriculum is designed to raise these dynamics and enable participants to identify them and work to avoid them.

This curriculum contains six 1-hour to 1½-hour sessions. The first and last sessions frame the conversation with theological and ethical issues. The middle four sessions highlight specific issues confronting adolescents today: sexual harassment, dating violence including date rape, incest, pornography, and abusive images found in some popular media, including MTV and other music video.

Preparing for This Course

READING

There are several things you can do to prepare for teaching with this curriculum. First, do some reading on the subject. *Love Does No Harm: Sexual Ethics for the Rest of Us,* by Rev. Marie Fortune, is especially recommended. This book and many other helpful ones are listed in Resources. We have tried to provide as much information as possible within the curriculum so that it may be taught by persons whose levels of knowledge differ. However, any additional experience that you can bring to the course will be extremely useful. The effectiveness of this course is greatly increased by your ability to convey the information clearly and to answer questions thoughtfully. Some extra reading will aid in this as well.

LEADERSHIP/TEACHING STYLE

It is recommended that this course be taught with at least one man and one woman leading. If this is not possible, recruit adult discussion leaders of both genders for help with each session. We also recommend that you reflect on the way in which this course is taught. As regards the manner of teaching, we would highlight two things.

The first is a strong belief that this course be an interactive experience. By this we mean that the curriculum is designed to be built around discussion as much as possible. Avoid a lecture-style format in favor of one that includes participants in the learning process. Ask them to talk with one another and to grapple with the material together. Although there will be times that discussion is difficult to start or maintain, we hope you will persevere and not always want to provide the "answers." Of course, this is balanced by the need to make sure that no incorrect or harmful information goes unchallenged. Clearly, you as a leader need to strike a balance by conveying all the important information included here and facilitating participants in generating their own understandings and perspectives on the material. One book that might be of help is Parker Palmer's *To Know As We Are Known: Education as a Spiritual Journey* (Harper San Francisco, 1993).

The second issue regarding teaching style is the need for good boundaries on the part of the leader. Oftentimes youth leaders are young seminarians who may be less than ten years older than some of the teenagers. This closeness in age can cause confusion and blur boundaries between pastor and parishioner. Even if the leader is not close in age, it may be difficult to keep roles clearly defined. But it is imperative that the leader of this course, or any church worker, keep a very clear sense of her/his position. In this context that means that you are teacher, mentor, supporter, and guide. It should go without saying that you are not to be involved romantically with students. As a leader, you are in a position of authority in relation to the members of your youth group. You have more power than they and you are responsible for using it in their best interest. In short, you have the responsibility to model healthy relationship with the group.

NETWORKING

It would be helpful to contact your local rape crisis center, battered women's shelter, or any other agency or person, either local or national, who might serve as a resource. Many denominations have people working nationally on this issue and they would be helpful as well. This kind of networking helps you in at least two ways: in your presentation of the material and in your ability to respond to a participant if she/he discloses that she/he is a survivor of sexual abuse/violence.

DEALING WITH SURVIVORS

The use of this course may encourage some of the group members to report experiences of sexual assault or abuse to you. Be prepared for this; investigate local resources. We strongly recommend that you have a contact person at your local rape crisis center and at the children's protective services agency in your area. If you're struggling to discern whether or not to report, we have included an article in the appendix that may be helpful. We recommend that you read it. Also, know both your local and denominational church's policy. In short, the best thing you can do is think ahead and have a plan of action. (One resource that is particularly helpful in thinking about the issues involved in reporting, the value of this kind of education, and the best way that the church can respond to abuse are the videos entitled *Hear Their Cries: Religious Responses to Child Abuse* and *Bless Our Children: Preventing Sexual Abuse*. For rental information, see Resources.)

If someone comes to you, believe them. If the abuse is continuing, assure them that you will help them take appropriate action to stop the abuse and you will help them deal with their feelings about it. Encourage the teenager to report the assault or abuse to a sexual assault agency. If the abuse happened in the past, let them know that you will help them find resources for their healing process. In either case, have some of the books listed in Resources available to lend if someone comes to you.

INVOLVING YOUNG PEOPLE

As you begin to outline when and how you are going to teach this course, it would be helpful to involve some of the young people from the group that you will be teaching. In fact, meeting with the group as a whole to talk with them about the course allows them some ownership of the process and can help with their interest in and ability to learn from the information presented in the curriculum.

PARENTS' MEETINGS

As you prepare for this course, we strongly recommend that you meet with parents. This provides an opportunity for parents to be educated first and alerted to some of the things their children will be learning. They will then be better prepared to respond to the questions and concerns the young people voice. Such a meeting also provides an opportunity for parents to raise any questions about the content of the course. Material on sexual abuse may raise some parents' concerns and resistance about sexuality education. A clear explanation of what will be presented usually addresses the concerns and minimizes resistance. Most parents are grateful that their children will be getting this important information and are supportive of the course.

We also recommend that parents *not* attend the sessions with their children.

INVOLVING YOUR PASTOR

As you prepare for this course, it is helpful to talk with your pastor or pastors and inform them of your process. You may want to invite them to meet with the youth group and/or parents. If the pastors are supportive and willing, a sermon about sexual abuse and why the church needs to address it is very helpful in laying the groundwork for a course such as this.

SESSION 1

God's Gift of Sexuality

OBJECTIVES

- To help participants understand that our bodies and sexuality are gifts from God
- To help participants understand that even though sexuality is a gift, it can be used to hurt someone deeply
- To help participants develop an understanding of their responsibility regarding their own sexuality so that they don't hurt someone else
- To help participants recognize that if they are victimized, it's not their fault

RESOURCES NEEDED

- Newsprint and marker, chalkboard and chalk, or overhead and marker
- Bibles for all participants
- If possible, a survivor who is a member of the church or community to tell his/her story (see "When Violence and Sexuality Are Confused" at the end of this session)

THE SESSION IN BRIEF

Getting Started
Introduce the Course (15 min)

Developing the Session
Discuss Sexuality and Bodies (20 min)
Violence (20 min)
When Violence and Sexuality Are Confused (20 min)
Concluding the Session (10 min)

BACKGROUND FOR THE LEADER

This session, and the entire course, is based on the belief that sexuality and violence are two very different things. God blessed us with the gifts of bodiliness and sexuality. God created us with longings for intimacy and connectedness with one another. A sexual relationship can be one expression of deep intimacy and love. But our sexuality is more than what we do genitally. Our sexuality is "the divine invitation to find our destinies not in loneliness but in deep connection."[1]

Contrasted to this is violence. Violence is the antithesis of connection and intimacy. It destroys trust. It violates and degrades.

In the past, although sexuality and violence have been seen as opposites, they were still seen as related. Rape/sexual violence is at one end of the spectrum; "normal" sexual activity is at the other. In other words, rape is seen as sex that just "got out of hand."

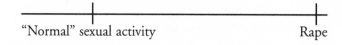

"Normal" sexual activity   Rape

1

In this curriculum, we suggest a different model. In this model, healthy sexuality and sexual abuse/violence are on different continuums. They are seen as being completely different.

CONTINUUM I: HEALTHY SEXUAL ACTIVITY = CONSENSUAL

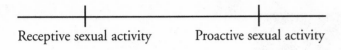

Receptive sexual activity   Proactive sexual activity

CONTINUUM II: SEXUAL ABUSE/VIOLENCE =
NONCONSENSUAL

Coercion   Use of physical force[2]

Although it may seem self-evident that sex and violence are completely different, our society confuses the two. We are taught that "good" sex is violent and that violence is sexy. We are taught that our sexuality is about dominance and submission. For men this means being taught that, to be a man, we need to be in control, get what we want, no matter what. For women, this means to be taught that we have no choice, whatever someone does to us is okay.

This course takes as its fundamental premise the belief that intermingling of sex and violence is wrong and is, ultimately, harmful. It leads to sexual violence that can deeply hurt or destroy its victims. Thus, we begin by differentiating between the two.

GETTING STARTED

Introduce the Course

Begin the session by asking members of the group to state their expectations about the course. If there are visitors or if those in the group do not know one another, some get-acquainted techniques should be used. Examples of this might include breaking into pairs and having each person talk for three minutes. When each has spoken, bring the group back together and have each person introduce his/her partner.

Be aware of individual responses, especially from males. They often will discount any interest or concern on their part. They may say they don't need to know about sexual assault. Be ready to use examples throughout the course that help to focus their awareness on the

fact that males can also be victims. (One such example is that one in seven boys is sexually abused by age eighteen and that 10 percent of reported rapes are of boys and men.[3])

In addition, note the responses of any participants who may be survivors of sexual violence. Given the statistics, it is very likely that such persons will be present. Tell the group that you will be available throughout the course to talk if anyone needs it. If possible, give them your phone number if you are an available resource. Also, be prepared with local resources.

Go over the session plans briefly, clarifying which of their expectations you intend to meet. Be very clear with participants that the subject matter being discussed is important and can be painful. Tell them that, because of this, it is very important that everyone respect the other members of the group. This means listening to others, not making fun of what another person has said, paying attention to whoever is speaking, and keeping confidential things that are said in the group.

Ask participants to list any other guidelines that will help them feel safer and more comfortable.

DEVELOPING THE SESSION

Discuss Sexuality and Bodies

1. Ask the group to name adjectives that describe sexuality and bodies. List the words and phrases the group provides on newsprint, chalkboard, or an overhead projector. Examples may be "negative"—dirty, sinful, bad, etc.—or "positive"—fun, sexy, beautiful, etc. Others may be functional, such as strong, fast, fat, thin, etc.

2. Have seven members of the group each read two verses of Song of Songs 2:8–17 and 4:1–4. Try to divide the readers equally among female and male.

3. On another sheet of newsprint, on another overhead transparency, or alongside the list on the chalkboard, ask the members of the group to list the adjectives that describe bodies and sexuality in the passage.

4. Talk together about the passages. Discuss the fact that these passages describe pleasure and love as positive things and names our maleness and our femaleness, our bodies, our sexuality as good. How does this compare with the list they made at the beginning?

5. Using the words that participants have provided from the text and the definition from the "Background for the Leader" section, identify sexuality as being essentially about connection, with God and with one another.

Violence

1. Ask participants to list words that define violence. List the words and phrases the group provides on newsprint or chalkboard.

2. Have six members of the group each read two verses of 2 Samuel 13:7–19. If there are enough people in the group, try to select different readers from the ones who read from Song of Songs. Again, the readers should be equally males and females if possible.

3. Ask the group to discuss the passage. (You may want to acknowledge that this is a very difficult text to read and a hard one to talk about.) What do they think it says? How is the relationship described here different from that described in Song of Songs?

4. Using the words the group formulated, the discussion about 2 Samuel, and the information from the "Background for the Leader" section, discuss what violence is.

5. Note for participants that violence and sexuality are very different things. Ask them to compare the two lists. What do they see? What is the primary difference?

NOTE TO THE LEADER

The primary difference to be highlighted is the element of choice. Violence is the use of power over someone else, against his/her will. It harms because it can inflict physical pain, but it also harms because it degrades and violates another's humanity. The gift of sexuality from God is based upon respect for the other, mutuality, equality, and honesty. It is about having the power to choose what is wanted and unwanted.

6. Share the two continuums with participants.

7. Refer to the list from the beginning of the session. Ask participants where "negative" words about sexuality come from. Point out that sexuality is a gift from God, but that when we confuse it with violence, it can be a very hurtful thing.

When Violence and Sexuality Are Confused

1. If you are able, have someone who has survived sexual abuse come to the course and tell her/his story to the group. (If a woman speaks of her experiences, be prepared to remind participants that boys and men are abused, too. You may want to read Brian's story as well. If the survivor is a man, remind participants that women are abused as well. Perhaps read Deborah's story.) If a visiting adult survivor is not possible, read the following two stories.

When Deborah was fifteen, she had her first date. Jason was sixteen and one of the cutest guys in the sophomore class. Deborah was really excited to go out with him. He had just gotten his driver's license and told her he would pick her up for a movie. On the way there, *all* Jason talked about was his sword collection. He never asked Deborah any questions. During the movie, Jason kept trying to feel Deborah's breasts. After the movie, Jason drove to a deserted street and forced Deborah to have intercourse.

One day after practice, Brian's coach asked him into his office. He told Brian he was making him starting quarterback. Brian was thrilled. Then the coach told Brian that his wife was away for the weekend and he was going to try and get some work done. He asked if Brian could stop by to talk over some plays with him. Brian said sure, he'd love to. When he got to the coach's house they started talking about plays, but then the coach told him he was tired of it and asked if Brian would like to watch movies with him. Brian said yes, but was shocked when they were pornographic movies. Later, his coach began touching him sexually. When it was over, the coach told him that if he told anyone, he wouldn't be a starter anymore and that the coach would tell everyone that Brian was gay.

NOTE TO THE LEADER

Any story about a male sexually abusing another male usually brings up reactions from participants about the offender or the victim being gay. (In fact, this is one of the biggest barriers to reporting by boys who have been victimized by men. They are afraid people will think they are gay.) It is important to remind participants that Brian's coach is married to a woman. In fact, most men who molest children, either boys or girls, are heterosexual. They molest children out of a desire to control them.

A second reminder to share with participants is that violence and sexuality are very different things. What Brian's coach did was violence. It had nothing to do with Brian's sexuality. Being molested by someone does not create your sexual orientation. If someone molests you, they perpetrate violence against you. It is, by definition, against your will. Therefore, it is not about the choices you have or will make regarding who you want to be involved with.

A third piece of information to share with participants regards gay and lesbian relationships. Although the above two stories portray heterosexual offenders, sexual abuse does happen within gay and lesbian relationships. It is as painful as any abuse perpetrated within heterosexual relationships and, because of the homophobia that exists in our society, it is much less likely that victims will report.

2. Ask if participants know people like Deborah and Brian or if they know of other stories. Ask how they think Deborah or Brian felt—what would they do, who could they tell? Do they think that either really had a choice? Why or why not?

3. Share with participants that you know these are hard stories to hear. Remind them that you are available to talk afterwards if they need to.

4. Discuss with participants the importance to talk about these kinds of things in church. You may want to refer to the section titled "Purpose of This Course" at the front of the book for information useful to this discussion.

CONCLUDING THE SESSION

1. Ask participants to make a collage that expresses their feelings about sexuality and violence. They might put their names in the middle of a piece of paper and surround it with pictures or images that best relate how they feel about sexual violence or, perhaps, they might make a collage showing how they think sexuality and violence differ.

2. Using their collages, ask participants to summarize what they learned from today's discussion. If they are having difficulty, share the following: sexuality is a gift from God and is good. It is our desire to be connected with other people and with God. Violence is destructive, it degrades and demeans and keeps us separate from one another and from God. Sometimes we confuse sexuality and violence. When this happens, people get hurt. This course is designed to help them learn what happens when sexuality and violence are mixed and how to stop it. The course is also intended to help if someone has been hurt by another's violence.

(If participants are willing, collect the collages and hang them up each week during class time. Be sure to take them down during the week to keep confidential what has been discussed.)

3. Remind participants that you are available to talk after class or, if you are able, during the week. Thank them for their cooperation and their willingness to talk about important but difficult things.

4. Share with them that next week's session will focus on sexual harassment.

SESSION 2

The Powerful and the Vulnerable: Sexual Harassment

OBJECTIVES

- To help participants understand sexual harassment
- To provide participants with an understanding of power as contextual and relational
- To help participants distinguish between "power over" and "power with"
- To help participants understand that they can both have power and be vulnerable

RESOURCES NEEDED

- Newsprint and marker, overhead projector and markers, or chalkboard and chalk
- VCR, TV, and video *Out of Bounds* (order in advance and preview; see Resource section)
- Collages from last week, if you were able to collect them

THE SESSION IN BRIEF

Getting Started
Build Community (5 min)

Developing the Session
Power and Vulnerability (30 min)
Sexual Harassment (10 min)
Video: *Out of Bounds* (20 min)
Discussion Questions (15 min)
Concluding the Session (10 min)

BACKGROUND FOR THE LEADER

1. This session is built around the concepts of power and vulnerability. However, it is important to define what is meant by these terms because we use them in a way that may differ from common understanding.[1]

Power, as used here, has two very important components: relational and contextual.

Power as Relational: Power is not an absolute trait, like skin color or height; it is relative. Person A may have power in relation to person B but not in relation to person C. That is why it is inaccurate to simply say that someone "has power" or "is powerful."

Power as Contextual: A person's power or lack of it is not a constant but varies with the context. A twenty-year-old man may be more powerful than a thirteen-year-old girl but his professor is more powerful than he.

RESOURCES CHART

	Sources of Power	Sources of Vulnerability
Age	older (or adulthood)	youth (or simply younger)
Gender	male	female
Race	Caucasian	Asian/Pacific Islander, African American, Native American, Hispanic, and other people of color
Role	teacher, coach, parent	student, player, child
Sexual Orientation	heterosexual	lesbian, gay, bisexual
Physical Resources	ability, large physical size, physical strength	disability, small size, physical weakness
Economic Resources	wealth, job skills	poverty, lack of job skills
Intellectual Resources	knowledge, access to information	lack of these
Psychological Resources	breadth of life experience	inexperience, lack of coping skills
Social Resources	support, friends, family	isolation

Both of these concepts rest on the idea that power is a measure of one person's (or a group's) resources as compared to another person's (or a group's) resources. Those who have greater resources than others have power relative to them; those who command fewer resources are vulnerable relative to them.

It is important to note that resources can be anything that can be a source of strength, anything that can be drawn upon to take care of a need or be used to one's advantage. The chart above illustrates the situation in the United States and may help clarify this idea.

Thus, as we see:

Power = Greater resources
Vulnerability = Fewer resources

The other important distinction about power is that of its use. Power can be used to control or manipulate. This might be defined as "power over." Power can also be defined as the capacity to do things or make things happen, to act, including on behalf of others. This is "power to do/make" or "power with."

Examples of this distinction are:

"POWER OVER"	"POWER WITH"
To control others (e.g., Brian's coach from Session 1)	To provide leadership (a coach who uses his/her role to guide the team with genuine care for the players)
To preserve privilege and power of gender, race, body size, etc. (e.g., Jason, from Session 1, used his body size and power as a male to get what he wanted)	To respect and protect the vulnerable, i.e., those who have less power

2. The particular issue covered in this session is that of sexual harassment as defined by the U.S. Federal Equal Employment Opportunity Commission:

The use of one's authority or power, either explicitly or implicitly, to coerce another into unwanted sexual relations or to punish another for his or her refusal; or the creation of an intimidating, hostile or offensive . . . environment through verbal or physical conduct of a sexual nature.

GETTING STARTED

Build Community

Ask participants:
- What are the main things you remember from the last session? (If you have put the collages up again, you may want to ask participants to refer to them.)
- Are there any questions or comments you now have about the session?
- Do you remember the guidelines of respect that were outlined last week?

DEVELOPING THE SESSION

Power and Vulnerability

1. Ask participants to define both power and vulnerability and list their responses on newsprint, the chalk-

board, or an overhead. Clarify, using the information provided in the "Background for the Leader" section. Be sure to highlight for participants the concept of resources. (It might be helpful to have an overhead or have the definitions on a piece of newsprint or on the chalkboard.)

2. Have the Resources Chart given in "Background for the Leader" section either as an overhead or drawn on newsprint or a chalkboard.

3. Go over this chart. If participants have questions about race or gender, talk with them about how our society discriminates against people of color and women and that this is why white people and men have a resource in their race and their gender. Note that this is the current situation; it doesn't make it fair or right.

4. Ask participants to think of concrete examples of some of the categories, especially the ones having to do with physical, economic, intellectual, and other resources. For instance, if I am in a wheelchair and you don't have any disabilities, you have more power than I do.

5. Have the group do two (brief) role plays. In each role play, ask two members of the group to stand up. Then ask the group to describe each of the following relationships:

- One in which one person has more power than the other
- One in which the power seems to be relatively equal between the two

Describe to the actors the roles they are to play. For example: "John, pretend that you are Mr. Jones, the basketball coach. Mary, pretend you're on the basketball team." Then ask John, as Mr. Jones, to say something to Mary that illustrates his power in relation to her. For example, he might tell her to run ten laps. Ask Mary to respond to Mr. Jones in a way that illustrates his power in relation to her. To illustrate the relationship where the power is equal, you could ask the two people to pretend that they are best friends of the same age and race.

6. Ask participants to name other examples of relationships between people where one person has more power than another and relationships in which people are relatively equal in power.

7. Use the following examples and ask participants to discuss who is more powerful and who is more vulnerable in each.

- A 14-year-old African American girl and a 17-year-old Hispanic boy who are dating
- A 16-year-old white boy and his 40-year-old white male teacher

- A 14-year-old Asian American girl and her 15-year-old Asian American friend who is also a girl

In the first situation, the resources of race are equal, but the boy has both gender and age as resources to make him more powerful. In the second situation, two white males have equal resources in these areas, but the teacher has both age and role as resources so he is more powerful. In the third situation, both are girls, both are Asian, and, although their age is somewhat different, their resources are almost equal; therefore, their power is equal.

8. Introduce the concept of "power over" and "power with." Ask participants to give examples of people who have more power in a given situation using it as "power over." Then ask them to give examples of situations of "power with."

9. Share with participants that you are now going to talk about a specific issue that involves power and how it is used.

Sexual Harassment

1. Introduce the concept of sexual harassment. Ask participants what they think it means.

2. Share the definition given in the "Background for the Leader" section. Discuss it with the group. The main concept is that someone uses his/her power (resources) over and against someone else in order to control or manipulate them.

Video: *Out of Bounds*

Show *Out of Bounds*. (Ordering information is in the Resource section.) The video illustrates sexual harassment and provides material for further discussion. If possible, discuss the video in separate groups of the same sex with an adult leader of the same sex for each group. Bring the groups together and share reactions. Begin discussion using the questions suggested. If time allows, role play other responses to the situation portrayed in the video.

Out of Bounds portrays a group of high-school-aged boys who harass a girl with both words and touch. It is narrated by a man in his twenties who clarifies the dynamics throughout the video. The message is that harassment is about power and attitude. The video uses a fairly multicultural cast and is usable for most audiences.

Discussion Questions

- Was the situation real to you? Does this ever happen in your school?
- What things did Gus and Juan, and later Gus, Juan, and Kyle, do? Do you ever do things like this?
- Why did the narrator say it was about "power" and "attitude"?
- How did Freddie respond to Gus, Juan, and Kyle? How might you respond if someone sexually harassed you?
- Ask them if their school has a sexual harassment policy.
- Ask for further questions.

CONCLUDING THE SESSION

1. Ask participants if they have any questions.

2. Emphasize that if sexual harassment happens to members of the group, it is important to tell an adult they trust. Remind them that you are available to talk if they need to. If you know of local resources for people who have been sexually harassed, share them with the group.

3. Describe plans for the next session.

The Good, the Bad, and the Confusing

OBJECTIVES

- To increase participant's knowledge of good/safe, bad/unsafe, and confusing touch
- To increase participant's knowledge of child sexual abuse

RESOURCES NEEDED

- 3" x 5" note cards
- Newsprint and marker, chalkboard and chalk, or overhead projector, transparencies, and markers

THE SESSION IN BRIEF

Getting Started
    Build Community (5 min)
Developing the Session
    Defining Good/Safe, Bad/Unsafe, and Confusing Touch (20 min)
    Discussion: Right and Wrong of Touching (15 min)
    Child Sexual Abuse (5 min)
    Demonstrate Potential Abuse Situations (35 min)
    Discuss: What Is Wrong About Child Sexual Abuse? (10 min)
Concluding the Session (5 min)

BACKGROUND FOR THE LEADER

There are two areas to cover in this session.

1. The first regards touch. The following chart illustrates concepts developed by Cordelia Anderson called the Touch Continuum.[1]

GOOD, BAD, CONFUSING TOUCH

Touches can be good, bad, or confusing.

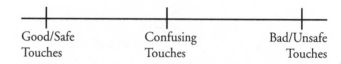

| Good/Safe Touches | Confusing Touches | Bad/Unsafe Touches |

Good/Safe Touches: Good/safe touches are touches that make the receiver feel affirmed—good about him- or herself. Good touches are experienced by the receiver as warm, caring, nurturing, supportive. They do not diminish the receiver; they do not take from the receiver. All persons need to receive this kind of touch.

Bad/Unsafe Touches: Bad/unsafe touches are those that hurt the receiver—touches that make the receiver feel bad about her- or himself, touches that inflict pain or that seem to disregard the receiver's feelings. It is usually very clear that the receiver does not want this kind of touching. Bad touches are experienced by the receiver as manipulative, coercive, abusive, frightening.

Confusing Touches: Confusing touches are touches that make the receiver feel uncomfortable, uneasy, confused, unsure. The receiver experiences confusion and conflicting feelings about the touch and/or about the person who does the touching. The intent of the toucher may be unclear, the touch may be unfamiliar. There are times when this kind of touch "feels good" but is also frightening, such as a touch that is sexually stimulating but initiated by an adult who tells the adolescent not to tell. Thus, touch that "feels good" is not always good/safe touch.

What determines the nature of a touch? Whether a touch is "good/safe," "bad/unsafe," or "confusing" is determined by how the receiver experiences it—*not* by the intentions of the person doing the touching. The "toucher" may intend the touch to convey a certain kind of message (support, affection, etc.); but the message is entirely dependent upon how the receiver perceives the touch, and the toucher has no control over this. *The toucher's intentions are irrelevant.*

The element of choice. Foremost in how the receiver experiences a touch is the element of choice: Does the receiver have a choice in the matter of whether to be touched? Is the touch offered or forced upon the receiver, perhaps on the assumption that the receiver wants to be touched? Is the receiver free to accept or decline the offer? Touch that is not freely chosen by the receiver is likely to be experienced as "bad/unsafe" or "confusing" touch.

If participants are having a hard time grasping "good/safe" and "bad/unsafe," perhaps "wanted" and "unwanted" may be more illustrative because the point of this information is that the quality of the touch depends on the receiver's experience of it, *not* on the intentions of the "toucher."

To clarify why it is that the intentions of the toucher are irrelevant in determining whether touch is good/safe, bad/unsafe or confusing,[2] it is useful to talk about the "filter" through which the receiver receives the touch. This filter determines how a touch is experienced. The following is a list of those things that serve as filters through which the receiver might experience a touch:

Receiver's freedom of choice about the touching	Receiver's current emotional state; receiver's perception of the toucher
Receiver's life situation	
Receiver's interests at the moment	Receiver and toucher's relationship
Receiver's history of abuse; receiver's experience with touch	Receiver's expectations for touch; receiver's feelings about touch in general
	Receiver's physical state, etc.[3]

Even as we discuss how touch can be harmful, it is essential to affirm the value of touch. Touching is valuable and necessary. In fact, without touch, young babies do not develop properly. This experience of touch deprivation is known as failure to thrive and can be deadly. Given its import, we do not want participants to draw the mistaken conclusion that since touching can be abusive, it should be avoided entirely. But unless we can name what is abusive or unwanted, we may be confused about the issue. Therefore, it is helpful to understand what determines whether a touch is good/safe, bad/unsafe, or confusing. This helps us to understand what we are experiencing and it helps us to be aware of how our touches are received by others.

2. The second area of information covered in this session is child sexual abuse. Child sexual abuse refers to a wide range of abuse perpetrated on children and teenagers by older or more powerful persons. It can include touching in sexual areas, forcing a child or teen to watch sexual movies or listen to sexual talk, forcing children or teens to pose for seductive or sexual photographs, forcing a child or teen to perform oral sex, rape, or other penetration, fondling, kissing or holding in an uncomfortable way, inflicting physical or sexual torture on a child, forcing a child or teen to watch sex acts or look at genitalia, bathing a child or teen in a way that is intrusive, objectifying or ridiculing a child or teen's body, encouraging or goading a child into unwanted sex, telling a child or teen she/he is only good for sex, involving a child or teen in prostitution or pornography.

As in last week's session, the fact of *power* is very important to emphasize here. Just as sexual harassment is about using your resources—your power—*over* someone else, so is child sexual abuse. Instead of using power *with* a child or teen to respect and protect, an abuser *violates* the child or teen.

This kind of abuse happens within the family as well as by outside perpetrators. When it is within the family, it is called incestuous abuse.

In their landmark book, *The Courage to Heal*, Ellen Bass and Laura Davis write:

> If you have been sexually abused, you are not alone. One in three girls, and one in seven boys, are sexually abused by the time they reach the age of eighteen. Sexual abuse happens to children of every class, culture, race, religion, and gender. Children are abused by fathers, stepfathers, uncles, brothers, grandparents, neighbors, family friends, baby-sitters, teachers, strangers, and sometimes by aunts and mothers. Although women do abuse, the vast majority of abusers are heterosexual men.[4]

GETTING STARTED

Build Community

Begin the session with community building. In order to reconnect the group, ask:

- What is the main thing you remember from the last session? Or, could someone summarize the last session?
- Are there any questions or comments you now have about the last session?

DEVELOPING THE SESSION

Defining Good/Safe, Bad/Unsafe, and Confusing Touch

1. Begin by asking participants to name different kinds of touches. Examples might be hugging, backrubs, handshakes, etc. If they haven't named any "bad" touches, include spanking, slapping, hitting, etc.

2. Ask participants what they think the difference is between these types of touches.

3. Explain briefly the concept of "continuum," used here to refer to gradations between extremes. For example, red, white, and shades of pink in between.

4. On a chalkboard, newsprint, or overhead transparency, draw the continuum listed below.

GOOD/SAFE   CONFUSING   BAD/UNSAFE

5. Using the explanations the participants provided above and the information from the "Background for the Leader" section, ask the group to define each of these. Write the definitions below each heading on the continuum. (Note: It is important to share with participants that the receiver's experience of the touch is the most important criteria for determining the kind of touch it is.)

Complete Sentence Fragments

1. Distribute blank 3" x 5" index cards to each group member. Working alone, ask them to complete the following sentences based on their current experience. Write one sentence fragment at a time on the board. Ask them to copy it and fill in their response. After participants have had time to respond, write the next one. Let them know that the cards will be handed in for use now but that their names will not be on them and their responses will be anonymous.

> I feel bad/unsafe when [someone touches me in a certain way].
> I feel good/safe when [someone touches me in a certain way].
> I feel confused when [someone touches me in a certain way].

Ask them to identify the "someone" by role, not by name, and describe the touch. For example:

> "I feel bad/unsafe when my mother slaps me."
> "I feel good/safe when my friend gives me a hug."
> "I feel confused when someone I don't know very well puts his arm around me."

2. Collect the cards. Sorting through quickly, read aloud the most representative examples of each type of touch. Be sure to use any examples of confusing and bad touch in the family. Write some examples on the continuum you have on the board or overhead.

NOTE TO THE LEADER

Using the response cards and reading the responses aloud helps break down the individual's sense of isolation: they hear their own experiences in others' responses and yet remain anonymous.

DISCUSSION: THE RIGHT AND WRONG OF TOUCHING

1. Ask participants to think about the responses they just gave to the Touch Continuum exercise and discuss more fully the concepts of good/safe, bad/unsafe, and confusing touch. The following questions are designed to help with the discussion. With each question are suggestions for you to highlight if participants are having difficulty responding.

What is wrong with "bad/unsafe" touch? "Bad/unsafe" touch makes a person feel bad. The person may feel frightened, powerless, put down, ripped off, and exploited because someone who is more powerful (has more resources) is touching the person in a particular way or forcing the person to do something she/he does not want to do. It is wrong to touch someone this way because it takes away that person's right to decide what is wanted and it lowers a person's sense of self-worth. It is using power "over" someone. It is not wrong because it is sexual; it's wrong because it is exploitative and takes advantage of the other person.

What is right about "good/safe" touch? "Good/safe" touch makes a person feel good about him- or herself. When someone touches another in a positive and nonexploitative way, the receiver feels affirmed, accepted, respected, supported, and loved. It is touch that both people freely choose. It is based on power "with."

Is "good/safe" touch always the right thing to do? It is important not to confuse "good/safe" touch with the "if it feels good, do it" philosophy. People may choose to be touched or to touch another in different ways at different times. (For elaboration on this idea, see the "Background for the Leader" for information on the receiver's "filter.") Circumstances will mean that some touch is appropriate and other touch is not. What may be "good/safe" touch in one relationship wouldn't be in another. For example, a French kiss may be appropriate with a girlfriend or boyfriend but not with an uncle. What may be "good/safe" touch at one point in a relationship may be "confusing" or "bad/unsafe" touch at a later point. For example, petting may be "good/safe" touch if it is mutually chosen. If one person does not

want to pet, then it becomes "confusing" or "bad/ unsafe" touch. "Good/safe" touch (by definition) is never wrong. However, it may not always be the wisest or most appropriate action.

So is "confusing" touch right or wrong? It is mostly confusing because it is never really clear what is going on or why someone is touching you in this way. If the person being touched feels in any way uncomfortable, frightened, or hesitant and really does not want to be made to feel this way, then it is wrong to touch them.

Sometimes the confusion occurs in an incestuous situation. Sexual attention from a parent figure may "feel good" to an adolescent but may also be uncomfortable or frightening. It is wrong for an adult to take advantage of an adolescent in this way. If he/she does, it is because he/she is abusing his/her power and using it "over" a child or adolescent.

2. From the above discussion, ask participants to name some guidelines that they would share with a friend who wasn't at this class about touch.

Examples might be:

- It is wrong to touch someone else in a way that takes advantage of the other person or is abusive. It is wrong to use your power "over" someone. If someone tells you that they don't want you to touch them, listen to them. Remember, even if you think your touch is good, it's how the other person receives it that's important.

- It is wrong for someone to touch you if you don't want to be touched that way or at that time. You do not have to tolerate being touched in any way that makes you feel bad or confused. You can and should decide who touches you and how they can touch you. If you don't like the way you're being touched or treated, you have the right to say what you want and don't want. Speak up.

- "No" means no and "yes" means yes. Be as clear and straightforward as you can.

- Sometimes, even when we feel that a touch is "bad/ unsafe" and we've been very clear by saying "no," the other person persists in touching us. Sometimes we're confused about a touch and another person coerces or forces us to do something. This is abusive, and when abuse happens to us in this way, it is never our fault. Whenever abuse happens, it is important to tell someone you trust.

3. Share with the group that you are now going to talk about a specific kind of touch and that they will be asked to use the ideas they learned above.

Child Sexual Abuse

1. Ask the group (do not divide into same-sex groups) to pretend that you are a stranger to this culture and to define for you the meaning of "child sexual abuse." List words and phrases on newsprint, an overhead transparency, or the chalkboard. If the group is having difficulty, add information from the "Background for the Leader."

Remind the group that children and adolescents can be abused by family members as well as by people outside their families. This kind of abuse is called incest.

2. Ask the group to list people who can abuse children or adolescents. Again, if the group is having difficulty, augment their responses with the information from the "Background for the Leader." Be sure to share with them that some women, including mothers, do abuse but that the most common abuse is by heterosexual men, including fathers, stepfathers, uncles, brothers, and grandfathers.

3. Share with participants that this is not an uncommon form of abuse. Give them the statistics from the information in the "Background for the Leader" section. Emphasize that it happens to boys as well as girls. Tell them that if it happens to them or someone they know, they are not alone and that there are people they can talk with.

Demonstrate Potential Abuse Situations

1. As a group leader, demonstrate two situations that might be faced by an adolescent. Go through each demonstration once with the potential victim playing a nonassertive, passive role. Discuss and problem-solve in the group, and repeat the situation with the victim being assertive and getting out of the situation.

NOTE TO THE LEADER

The demonstration should be done by the group leader(s). If you are the only group leader, invite another adult to assist you. Do not involve young people in acting out the situation. Such use of adolescents could too easily be misconstrued. It also puts them in an awkward situation with their peers. The demonstration will be effective if carried out by the group leader(s).

Demonstration 1: The potential victim (male or female, preferably male) goes into the bathroom and starts to undress in order to bathe. Having shut the door behind him (her), the door opens and an older brother comes in and just stands there watching. This has never happened to the younger sibling before.

Passive response: The adolescent is clearly uncomfortable but says nothing, waiting for the other person to leave. The older brother does not leave, so the adolescent gets up and leaves the room.

Assertive response: The adolescent says to the older brother: "I don't like you watching me. I want you to leave right now." When he leaves, he (she) locks the door. If he does not leave, he (she) puts on a robe and goes and tells a parent what the older brother is doing and asks help in stopping the brother's behavior.

Demonstration 2: The potential victim (female) has just come home from her youth fellowship meeting. Her father is home alone, sitting in the living room watching TV. When she comes in the house, her father calls her into the living room and tells her to come over and sit on his lap. She has been sitting on her father's lap since she was a child, but now she has become uncomfortable with his touching behavior. She hesitates. This has happened before and she knows what to expect. But she sits on his lap and he holds her tight and tries to kiss her on the mouth. She feels uncomfortable, confused, and frightened.

Passive response: She is clearly uncomfortable and tries to pull away from him but does not succeed. She tells no one about his sexual advances toward her.

Assertive response: She pulls away, stand up and says, "I don't like you to touch me this way. I want you to stop." She then leaves the room and tells someone what has been happening (her mother, a teacher at school, a Sunday School teacher, etc.).

Discuss: What Is Wrong About Child Sexual Abuse?

Ask participants to share what they think is wrong about child sexual abuse. Discuss their ideas, going back to the discussion of power and "bad" touch.

NOTE TO THE LEADER

1. Emphasize that abuse is not wrong because it is sexual. Rather it is wrong because it involves one person who is older and more powerful taking advantage sexually of a person who is younger and vulnerable. The victim is manipulated or coerced or is too confused to know what to do and so goes along with the sexual activity, not seeing any alternative.

2. When the sexual contact takes place between an adult male and an adolescent male, this does not mean that either the offender is gay or that the adolescent victim will "become" gay because of the contact. It is not wrong because it is sexual contact between persons of the same gender but because of the exploitation of the young person.

3. Sexual contact per se is not wrong. Any adult taking advantage of a child or adolescent sexually is behaving irresponsibly and illegally. This is a betrayal of the adult role of protector or caretaker who, misusing authority, coerces the adolescent into sexual activity. The adolescent feels exploited and used by the adult for sexual gratification. The adolescent may be confused by or ambivalent about feeling uncomfortable with the adult's sexual approach. The young person will be especially confused about the difference between sexual activity and affection.

4. Up until now, we have been discussing how participants might be victims of child sexual abuse. It is important to stress that they need to be aware of the way in which they treat the children for whom they babysit and their own siblings. Remind the group about the discussion of resources and how there are situations where they will be more powerful than someone else.

CONCLUDING THE SESSION

1. Ask if there are any questions or comments.
2. Remind participants that you are available to talk afterwards.
3. Describe plans for the next session.

SESSION 4

The Danger of the Dreamworlds

OBJECTIVES

- To increase participants' awareness of the representation of men and/or women as sex objects and of violence used in the media, particularly MTV, as sources of stereotypes and values about women, men, and relationships
- To increase participants' skill at evaluating the messages portrayed in advertising and music videos, especially MTV, that use images of sexual or physical violence

RESOURCES NEEDED

- Newsprint and markers, overhead and markers, or chalkboard and chalk
- VCR, TV, and the video *Dreamworlds II* (order in advance and preview)

THE SESSION IN BRIEF

Getting Started
Build Community (5 min)
Developing the Session
Sources of Values (10 min)
Define Stereotypes (10 min)

Show Video: *Dreamworlds II* (55 min)
Discussion Questions (15 min)
Concluding the Session (5 min)

BACKGROUND FOR THE LEADER

This course takes as a basic premise that we live in a society that discriminates against and oppresses people including women, people of color, gay men and lesbian women, people with disabilities, etc.[1] As we have seen in the Resources Chart in Session 2, such oppression means that members of an oppressed group are vulnerable vis-à-vis the group that oppresses them. The opposite is true as well, members of a group that oppresses another are more powerful vis-à-vis that group.

This session seeks to highlight the ways in which sexism (discrimination against and oppression of women) is integrally linked to sexual violence.

GETTING STARTED

Build Community

Begin the session with community building. In order to reconnect the group, ask:

15

- What is the main thing you remember from last session?
- Are there any questions or comments you now have about the last session?

DEVELOPING THE SESSION

Sources of Values

1. Ask the group to brainstorm about where they learn what to wear, what music to listen to, how to do their hair, how to act, etc. Write "clothes," "music," "hair," "act" on the newsprint, overhead, or chalkboard and list answers from the participants under the appropriate heading.

2. If they haven't mentioned it yet, ask if they look at magazine ads and music videos to find out how to dress, etc.

3. Share that today we're going to focus on how ideas about how we should dress, what music to listen to, how to do our hair, etc., are shaped by the larger culture, especially advertising and music videos.

Define Stereotypes

1. Ask the group in general to define a stereotype.

NOTE TO THE LEADER

If the group is having trouble, or hasn't come up with the following, be sure to add it to their list: "A stereotype is a commonly held image of or belief about people or things as a group, usually not based on fact or reality; that is, the belief or image is often false or a negative misinterpretation of some truth."

2. Ask participants for examples of stereotypes. List them on the chalkboard, overhead transparency, or newsprint. Examples might include: "All blondes are dumb"; "all football players have a low IQ"; "men are always stronger than women."

3. Share with participants that today's discussion focuses on the way in which the media and advertising uses stereotypes of what it means to be a man and a woman.

Show Video: Dreamworlds II

Show the video *Dreamworlds II: Desire, Sex, and Power in Music Video* to illustrate how images about men and women and relationships are affected by advertising and much of what is shown on MTV as well as to provide material for further discussion. Note that *Dreamworlds II* lasts 55 minutes and will take most of the session. This may seem like a lot of time to spend on one piece, but the information provided makes it time well spent. Following the video, stay in the large group and discuss the suggested questions.

This is a documentary video, made for teens and adults, that makes a convincing and very alarming case for the idea that images of women and male-female relationships common to advertising and music video promote objectification of women, violence, and rape. It should be noted that this video contains material from MTV that is explicit. There is no nudity, but the videos examined show sexually explicit scenes. Toward the end, *Dreamworlds II* splices between the rape scene from the movie *The Accused* and music videos.

Although this may seem too much for teenagers, it is important to use because teenagers (and children much younger) watch MTV and other music video stations regularly. It is a main source of information and, as we see in the video, values for them.

The leader is advised to alert the group to the difficult subject matter, especially the rape scene, and to give them permission to leave the room if they need to.

Discussion Questions

- Which video segments were familiar? Can you give other examples of video segments that illustrate the same problem?
- What things do these video segments say are important, what values do they express? (Example: Men must be strong and have a woman.) Ask the group to identify characteristics of a "real man" and a "real woman" according to the videos. List on newsprint, overhead transparency, or chalkboard. For example:

"REAL MAN"	"REAL WOMAN"
• strong	• young
• tough	• not fat
• in control	• sexy
	• likes to take clothes off
	• always wants sex
	• likes to be controlled

- How do these images relate to the people you know? If you are male, how do you compare with the males in these videos? If you are female, how do you compare with the females in these videos?
- How do the relationships compare to what you want in a relationship?
- Now that you've seen *Dreamworlds II*, what do you think about watching music videos or looking at advertisements to get ideas about how to dress, act, etc.?

CONCLUDING THE SESSION

1. Ask participants to look at advertisements and/or watch music videos this week with the above discussion in mind. Also ask them to look at computer games to see if they find similar things.

2. Ask the group if they have any other questions.

3. Remind participants that you are available to talk afterwards if they want or need to.

SESSION 5

This Is Violence, Not Love

OBJECTIVES

- To increase participants' knowledge of acquaintance/date rape and dating violence
- To help participants recognize the relationship between diminishment, intimidation, and rape

RESOURCES NEEDED

- Newsprint and markers, chalkboard and chalk, or overhead transparencies and markers
- VCR, TV, and video *Scoring: Date Rape* (order video in advance and preview; see Resource section)

THE SESSION IN BRIEF

Getting Started
  Build Community (5 min)
Developing the Session
  Defining Rape (10 min)
  Date/Acquaintance Rape (15 min)
  Identifying Images of Rapist and Victim (15 min)
  The Sexual Abuse Continuum (15 min)
  Video: *Scoring: Date Rape* (20 min)
  Discussion: What Each of Us Needs to Know (20 min)
Concluding the Session (5 min)

BACKGROUND FOR THE LEADER

This session is designed as the culmination of the previous four sessions. It draws upon concepts that have already been presented and uses them to illustrate the dynamics at work in dating violence. In preparation for this session, it is recommended that the leader review Sessions 1–4.

Teenagers today face serious problems. Gang violence, guns, drugs, and alcohol are all real and present dangers in their lives. Added to these is a problem that is not often talked about—dating violence:

Many teenagers have problems with violence in a relationship with a boyfriend or girlfriend. Several surveys asked students in high school or college if they had been hit or sexually assaulted by someone they were dating or seeing. The survey showed that an average of 28 percent of the students experienced violence in a dating relationship.[1] That is more than one in every four students. In addition, studies show that 67 percent of young women reporting rape were raped in dating situations.[2]

As other recent books show, dating relationships are becoming increasingly violent. This session focuses on why this is happening and how we can help adolescents avoid violence or address it if it occurs.

The previous four sessions have illustrated that we

18

live in a culture that discriminates against women and teaches young women to desire dominance and submission (see Session 4). This means that too often teenagers are taught that asserting power over another is acceptable, even desirable, behavior. This leads to disregard of the other's personhood and can lead to bad/unsafe/unwanted touch. As young people are socialized into this culture, it is no wonder that these messages lead to dating violence.

This session seeks to highlight the ways in which teenagers can hurt other teenagers in dating relationships. There are several pieces of information needed for this session.

The first is the *definition of rape.*

Although legal definitions of rape vary from state to state, the most comprehensive definition refers to forced penetration by the penis or any object of the vagina, mouth, or anus against the will of the victim.[3]

In this definition, we see that rape is usually perpetrated by a man against a woman. However, about 10 percent of rape victims are men. In these cases, nearly all the perpetrators are also men. But women can rape, too, and it is important to share this fact. No matter what the circumstances, rape is a crime.

The second piece of information needed for this session is the *definition of date/acquaintance rape.*

In acquaintance rape, the rapist and victim may know each other casually—having met through a common activity, mutual friend, at a party, as neighbors, as students in the same class, at work, on a blind date, or while traveling. Or they may have a closer relationship—as steady dates or former sexual partners. Although largely a hidden phenomenon because it is the least reported type of rape (and rape, in general, is the most underreported crime against a person), many organizations, counselors, and social researchers agree that acquaintance rape is the most prevalent crime today.[4]

Here it is important to note that it doesn't matter what the relationship between the rapist and the victim is. It doesn't matter if the couple has had sex before, if they have dated for a long time, or if they have just met. Rape is defined by an act against another person's will. It is also important to note that, although we are focusing largely on heterosexual relationships, rape happens within gay and lesbian relationships as well. Rape happens when one person forces penetration on another against his or her will. It is a clear example of using one's power over another to harm them.

However, one of the most difficult dynamics in date/acquaintance rape is the fact that it is perpetrated by someone the victim knows. This can be deeply confusing. (Refer to the session on good/safe, bad/unsafe, and confusing touch.) Like child sexual abuse, date/acquaintance rape is an example of confusing touch (because it is done by someone the victim knows) but is an act that is painful to and disregards the victim's wishes and feelings. Thus, confusion sometimes arises in the victim as to whether a rape was actually committed. This is also true for the person who rapes someone he/she knows. He/she often mistakenly believes that he/she hasn't committed rape because of the mistaken belief that you can't rape someone you know. This is *not* true.

Another piece of information regarding date/acquaintance rape is that of *communication.* Although it may sound simple, one of the most difficult issues in date/acquaintance rape is that "no" is taken for "yes." This is fundamental to understanding both the power relationship and the Touch Continuum. If power is to be "with" another person and touch is to be "good/safe," then the people involved have to be clear about what they mean and have to listen to the other person. This means that if I say "no," I mean "no" and you need to listen. If you say "no," you need to mean "no" and I need to listen. Don't get into the "if she says 'no' she really means 'yes'" game. Everyone loses.

The third piece of information needed for this session has to do with the make-up of a rapist and a rape victim. Two often-asked questions are: Who rapes? And who gets raped?

Who gets raped is a fairly easy question to answer: anyone. However, rape victims/survivors are primarily women of any age, race, class, culture, educational background, profession. Babies as young as a few days old have been raped as have women in their nineties. As we have said before, men are also raped by other men. And, as we have seen in the session on child sexual abuse, male children can be rape victims as well.

Rape happens regardless of the specifics of its victim. Rape requires only three things:

Any person + Vulnerability + Rapist = Rape

Although we can decrease our vulnerability by learning about rape, ultimately, we can't eliminate it. Any of us can be in this position. Thus, it is important to emphasize that if a rape happens, *it is never the victim's fault*. Only the rapist is responsible when rape happens.

Who rapes is a much more difficult question to address. The best information we have indicates that, on the surface, men who rape appear no different from those who don't. Rapists come from every class, race, culture, educational background, and profession. One survey found that "about 8 percent of the men surveyed had raped or attempted to rape a woman sometime since the age of 14." The study goes on to say that the men who raped differed from the nonrapists in three ways:

1. They consumed more alcohol.
2. Their sexual values differed; i.e.:

   a. The rapists talked daily with their friends about "how a particular woman would be in bed" and they rated as "very frequently" how often they read *Playboy, Penthouse, Chic, Club, Forum, Gallery, Genesis, Oui,* or *Hustler* magazine.

   b. The men who raped said they approved of sexual intercourse under any circumstances, regardless of how long the man and woman have known each other.

   c. They were younger when they first had intercourse—age 15 as compared with age 17 for the nonaggressors.

3. They were more likely to believe rape-supportive myths: they saw women as adversaries, endorsed sex-role stereotyping, saw rape prevention as women's responsibility, and considered the mingling of aggression with sexuality as normal.[5]

Elaborating on numbers 2 and 3, there is evidence that rapists are men who adhere to societal stereotypes of what it means to be a man.

What differentiates men who rape women they know from men who do not is, in part, how much they believe the dogma of what most boys learn it means to be male—"macho" in the worst sense of the word.[6]

The fourth piece of information needed for this session is the Sexual Abuse Continuum (below).[7]

The purpose of this continuum is to help participants recognize that rape is not the only form of sexual abuse. Other behaviors lead to rape and can be very hurtful in and of themselves. They can create an environment of "power over" that harms those against whom the behavior is directed.

In the continuum we see that "Diminishment" is focused on making the other person feel bad about themselves. It puts the person "down" and gives the person criticizing or rating control of the situation. It is a form of sexual harassment. It is one step from "Intimidation," which is also harassing behavior. Intimidation also makes the person being harassed feel bad about him/herself, but utilizes fear as well so that not only does its victim(s) feel bad but also fearful as well. Both can be combined with "Force" and be used to set up a rape situation. Thus, each type of behavior supports the other.

The most important point to note is that abusive behavior encompasses more than rape. "Diminishment" and "Intimidation" behaviors are all abusive and need to be addressed.

GETTING STARTED

Build Community

Begin the session with community building. In order to reconnect the group, ask:

- Have any of you looked at advertisements or computer games or watched MTV and other music videos with new "eyes"?

DIMINISHMENT (PUT-DOWNS)	INTIMIDATION	FORCE
• Criticism of hair, body, clothes • Rating (e.g., male students lining the halls and holding up rating cards or fingers to evaluate female students who pass by). Racism is often a part of this—girls of color are rated lower than white girls.	• Spying on girl/boyfriend • Reading diaries of girl/boyfriend • Calling countless times to check on whereabouts • Threats of physical or sexual violence • Sexual gesturing in public	• Twisting arms • Poking with sharp objects such as penknife • Slapping • Punching • Isolating other person

• Are there any questions or comments you now have about the last session?

DEVELOPING THE SESSION

Defining Rape

1. Ask the group how their peers would define rape. List the words and phrases the group provides on newsprint, overhead transparency, or chalkboard. Examples of responses may include: sexual intercourse against one's will, fear-producing, forced, hurtful, violent.

2. Add any information from the "Background for the Leader" section. Highlight that rape is about force and takes place against the will of the victim. Also highlight that anyone can be a victim, including boys or men.

3. Remind the group of their discussion during the first session. Ask them to briefly name what sexuality is and what violence is. Point out to the group that rape is not about connecting or respecting or loving another person, it is violence. It hurts. It happens when one person uses his/her power "over" another.

Date/Acquaintance Rape

1. Ask the group to define date/acquaintance rape. Write the definition on the newsprint, overhead, or chalkboard. Fill in and/or clarify the definition using the information provided in the "Background for the Leader" section. Be sure to highlight that the relationship between the rapist and the victim is irrelevant. Regardless of whether the couple has had sex before, just met, or has been dating for a while, if one person forces another to have sex against her/his will, it's rape.

2. Remind participants about the Touch Continuum. Ask, "What kind of touch is date/acquaintance rape?" Briefly discuss, adding any information that needs to be raised from the "Background for the Leader."

3. Ask the group to think about their own experiences and the experiences of their friends. Using those experiences, ask them to think quietly about the following questions.

What happens on a date if one person wants to touch the other and that person says "no"?
Do they stop? Or do they keep going?
What do you mean when you say "no"?
What does it mean when your date says "no" or "I'm not sure"?

4. Discuss these questions briefly and share the information about communication from the "Background for the Leader" section. Be sure to emphasize that disregard of someone else's "no" means forcing them to do something they don't want to do. This is power over; this is bad/unsafe touch and could lead to rape.

Identifying Images of Rapist and Victim

1. Ask the group to call out words that describe a victim of rape. Write them on the chalkboard, overhead, or newsprint.

2. Ask the group to call out words that describe a rapist. Write these on the chalkboard, overhead, or newsprint.

3. Using the information from "Background for the Leader," clarify these definitions for the group. Emphasize that anyone can be raped (Any person + Vulnerability + Rapist = Rape). Also highlight how a person's thinking and values determines whether he or she will rape. Share with participants that this is precisely the reason for this class—to help reduce their vulnerability and to help them see the value in healthy relationships so that they can reduce their risk to harm others or to be harmed.

The Sexual Abuse Continuum

1. Draw the Sexual Abuse Continuum (from "Background for the Leader") on the chalkboard, overhead, or newsprint. List one example under each gradation on the continuum.

2. Ask participants to name more examples of each.

3. Ask participants if they know of people who have ever experienced any of the examples. That is, has anyone you know ever been "rated"?[8] Ask them how this makes people who have been rated feel.

4. Discuss together how each of these gradations are related to the others. Ask them how "diminishing" behavior, "intimidation," and "force" might lead to rape. Highlight that each is also hurtful in and of itself.

5. Ask them to watch for any of this kind of behavior in the video.

Show Video: Scoring: Date Rape

Show *Scoring: Date Rape* (ordering information provided in the Resource section) to illustrate date/acquaintance rape and to provide material for further discussion.

If possible, discuss the video in separate groups of the same sex each with an adult leader of the same sex. Then bring the groups together and share reactions. Begin discussion using the questions suggested. If time allows, role play other responses to the situations portrayed in the video.

Scoring: Date Rape

This video is the story of one guy who believes that dating is about "scoring" and "conquest." It portrays his pressuring his girlfriend and raping another woman. It also portrays one of his friends who accepts "no" for an answer. Throughout, a narrator highlights the mistakes he is making and shows the devastating impact a rape can have on a woman.

The story focuses on a white man but the cast is fairly diverse. We would recommend it for most audiences.

Discussion: What Each of Us Needs to Know

- Was this situation real to you? Does this happen in your school?
- Are there things that Jimmy believed that led him to behave the way he did? Can you give examples?
- What were some of the things that Jimmy did that Lionel and Tim told him were wrong?
- Why didn't Jimmy stop when Jesse said "no"?
- Do you understand why Jesse felt the way she did after Jimmy raped her? Explain.
- Are there things that Jimmy did that you think were "diminishing," "intimidating," or "forceful" either with Keri or Jesse?

1. Break the group into same-sex groups again with an adult leader of the same sex and ask them to generate a list of what they want males and females to understand about dating based on the information given in this session. Come back into the larger group and share the list.

2. Write "Males" and "Females" on newsprint, an overhead, or the chalkboard and list what participants say.

3. Fill out the list further with important points from the session including the following:

Males

- Understand that "no" means "no."
- Know it is never okay to force yourself on a girl or woman, even if you think she's been teasing and leading you on; even if you've heard that women say "no" but mean "yes"; even if you think it's "manly" to use force to get your way; even if you feel, physically, that you've "got to have sex"; even if she's drunk.
- Know that whenever you use force to have sex you are committing a crime called "rape" even if you know her; even if you've had sex with her before.
- Be aware of peer pressure to "score," work against it by listening to what your date is saying.
- Be aware of what society may tell you it means to be a "real" man, work against it by forming your own values based on respect, honesty, good listening, etc.
- Be aware of ways in which you may put down (diminish), intimidate, or use force with your date.
- Recognize that you can be raped too.

Females

- Say "no" when you mean "no"; say "yes" when you mean "yes"; stay in touch with your feelings to know the difference.
- Believe in your right to express your feelings and learn how to do so assertively.
- Be aware of stereotypes that prevent you from expressing yourself, such as "anger is unfeminine," "being polite, pleasant, and quiet is feminine."
- Be aware of specific situations in which you do not feel relaxed and "in charge." Sex-role stereotypes of passivity, submissiveness, and coyness are dangerous and can make one more vulnerable to sexual aggression.
- Be aware of the situations in which you are vulnerable and have fewer resources.
- Be aware of the ways in which you put down (diminish), intimidate, or force your date.

CONCLUDING THE SESSION

1. Ask if there are any questions or comments.
2. Remind the group that you are available to talk if anyone needs to.
3. Describe the plans for the next session.

SESSION 6

This Is About Love

OBJECTIVES

- To highlight what has been learned about sexual violence
- To help participants begin to distinguish healthy relationships from sexual violence

RESOURCES NEEDED

- Newsprint and markers or chalkboard and chalk
- 3" x 5" note cards and pencils
- Bibles for all participants

THE SESSION IN BRIEF

Getting Started
Build Community (5 min)
Developing the Session
Building a Healthy Sexual Ethic (65 min)
Concluding the Session (10 min)

BACKGROUND FOR THE LEADER

At the beginning of this curriculum, it was noted that a basic premise was that violence and sexuality are completely different things and that when they are confused, abuse and sexual violence follow. Sessions 3–5 highlighted how this is so.

As reiterated throughout, but especially in Session 4, this confusion is rampant in our society, as are sexual abuse and violence. This last session seeks to respond to this confusion and to this abuse by encouraging teenagers to begin to think about what healthy relationships are.

Although we cannot escape the socialization we receive in our society as men and women, we can fight against sexual violence by being clear about what healthy sexuality should be.

It is our belief that our sexuality is a deeply religious issue because sexuality is "the divine invitation to find our destinies not in loneliness but in deep connection."[1] Therefore, we need to be conscious of the decisions we make about our sexuality. And we need to root those decisions theologically and biblically.

This session focuses on helping participants do just that—to be conscious of their decisions regarding sexuality and to root them theologically.

Biblical and Theological Grounding

This is my commandment, that you love one another as I have loved you. No one has greater love than this, to lay down one's life for one's

23

friends. You are my friends if you do what I command you. I do not call you servants any longer, because the servant does not know what the master is doing; but I have called you friends, because I have made known to you everything that I have heard from [God]. You did not choose me but I chose you. And I appointed you to go and bear fruit, fruit that will last, so that [God] will give you whatever you ask in my name. I am giving you these commandments so that you may love one another. (John 15:12–17)

Owe no one anything except to love one another; for the one who loves another has fulfilled the law. The commandments, "You shall not commit adultery; You shall not murder; You shall not steal; You shall not covet"; and any other commandment, are summed up in this word, "Love your neighbor as yourself." Love does no wrong to a neighbor; therefore, love is the fulfilling of the law. (Romans 13:8–10)

In the first of these passages, John the Evangelist presents Jesus giving part of a farewell address to his disciples. The main theme Jesus offers them is that of friendship. If they are to live as he would have them live, they will love one another as lifelong friends love each other (the kind that would lay down their life for you).

In the second passage, the apostle Paul also seeks to give a summary speech. His conclusion is the same. The Law can be summed up in the statement "Love your neighbor as yourself." And he gives us a clue as to how to do this loving: we are not to wrong or harm our neighbor. Thus, to live in love, we must love ourselves and do no harm to our neighbor.

In both of these passages, we are given foundational statements about the Christian life. If we are able to love our neighbor as ourselves, we are following Christ and are living in accordance with God's law. We are also given clues as to how to live out this love: we are to seek to live with others as we would our best friend. This entails loving ourselves and doing harm to no one.

If these are the mandates for discipleship, they need also be the mandates for our intimate relationships. Thus, as we approach the task of trying to live out healthy relationships, our guiding principle is that of love—the love one would share with a best friend, rooted in love of self and seeking to do harm to no one.

GETTING STARTED

Build Community

Begin the session with community building. In order to reconnect the group, ask:

- Are there any questions or comments you now have about the last session?
- Share with participants that you know each of the previous sessions addressed difficult topics and that this session is geared toward formulating a positive response to these issues by helping us build healthy relationships

DEVELOPING THE SESSION

Building a Healthy Sexual Ethics

1. Put the heading "Sexual Abuse/Violence" on the board or newsprint. (Note: Overheads should not be used in this session because the sheets will need to be visible at the same time.) Ask participants to give examples from what they've learned in the previous five sessions.

2. Then put the heading "Healthy Relationship" next to "Sexual Abuse/Violence" on the board and ask participants to think about what a healthy relationship might look like. Examples of both might be:

SEXUAL ABUSE/ VIOLENCE	HEALTHY RELATIONSHIP
power over	power with
bad/unsafe, confusing touch	good touch
abuse/violation	mutuality/caring
disrespect	respect
controlling, getting own way	listening to other and working together
treating another like an object (e.g., Gus, Juan, and Kyle with Freddie, from *Out of Bounds*; Brian and his coach, from Session 1; Jimmy and Jesse, from *Scoring*.	sharing with an equal (e.g., Juan when he talked with Freddie and apologized)

3. In preparation for reading the scripture passages aloud, assign each participant a portion of John 15:12–17 and Romans 13:8–10.

4. Have the group read John 15:12–17 aloud. Ask participants what they think the passage is saying. Make a list on the board.

5. If they haven't mentioned it, note for participants the use of friendship as a model of discipleship. Write "Friendship" on the board or newsprint.

6. Pass out 3" x 5" notecards and ask participants to list five words that describe their best friend. Collect the cards. Read several examples from the cards and list them under "Friendship."

7. Read Romans 13:8–10 aloud. Ask participants what they think the passage is saying. Make a list on the board or newsprint.

8. If they haven't mentioned it, note the use of loving your neighbor as yourself and that Paul says the way to do this is not to harm anyone. Given these two precepts, Paul says that to love another, you must love yourself and do no harm.

9. Divide the group into several mixed-gender small groups (three or four people). Remind them of the differences between sexual abuse/violence and healthy relationships that they named. Remind them of John 15:12–17 and Romans 13:8–10. Based on these things, ask them to compose a "Bill of Rights"[2] for healthy relationships. This should contain ten principles that they would like to see in any relationship into which they enter. Tell them they have fifteen minutes to compose. Wander around and listen as groups discuss.

10. At the end of fifteen minutes, ask each group to write their "Bill of Rights" on the board and to tell the group why they chose the principles they did.

11. Using the examples given, combine the lists to form a class "Bill of Rights." Tell the group you will type up this list and get it to each of them. The list should include at least the following:

love of self (self-respect, etc.) and other	honesty
respect	mutuality
equality	no harm

CONCLUDING THE SESSION

1. Share the following with participants.

This entire course has been geared toward helping participants understand what sexual abuse and sexual violence are. The purpose of doing this kind of education is to help people make choices about their actions so that they can choose not to hurt others and so that they can reduce their own risk of being hurt. One of the most important steps in making choices away from abuse is knowing what is right and good in relationship.

This exercise of writing a "Bill of Rights" for healthy relationships is meant to help each person begin to think about what he/she wants to be and do in intimate relationships. It is not meant to be the final word, but the beginning of a lifetime of seeking to live in healthy relationships, as a disciple of Christ.

2. Ask if anyone has any questions.

3. Thank participants for their attention and respect during such an important discussion.

4. End with the following prayer or one of your own:

Gracious and loving Creator God, you have worked a miracle in each one of us present here today. You have made us in your image and created us with a desire to know you and to love, respect, and honor one another. For this marvelous gift, we praise you. We also ask your help today, God, because sometimes we misuse your gifts. Sometimes we hurt another person. Sometimes we ourselves are hurt. Help us to use all the learning you have given us here so that we can heal from the ways in which we have been hurt and so that we can act in ways that don't abuse or hurt other people. Be with us, we pray, in all that we do and say. In the name of Jesus Christ, who lived and loved with respect and honor. Amen.

Reporting Child Abuse: An Ethical Mandate for Ministry

Marie M. Fortune

The epidemic problem of child abuse in the United States (physical, sexual, and emotional) presents persons in ministry with a challenge and an opportunity. When child abuse is disclosed, the religious leader can intervene with sensitivity and compassion to bring an end to this suffering, which has most likely been chronic. Yet intervention by a minister is not necessarily forthcoming because of hesitancy, confusion, lack of information, and ambivalence. Situations of child abuse are complex, and a minister may well try a private solution and avoid using other community resources, usually to the detriment of the child and the family.

An Ethical Mandate

The ethical mandate for Christian ministry in response to the abused child is rooted in Jesus' gospel teachings. In Matthew, Jesus points to the child as the one who is the greatest in the kingdom:

Whoever receives one such child in my name receives me; but whoever causes one of these little ones who believe in me to stumble, it would be better for him to have a great millstone fastened

round his neck and to be drowned in the depth of the sea (Matt. 18:5–6, NRSV).

Jesus is consistent in his assertion of the specialness and value of children in a cultural context that regarded children as property of their fathers. He also points clearly to the responsibility of those around children to care for them.

This teaching must have been consistent with Jesus' understanding of the Hebrew custom of hospitality, in which the orphan, widow, and sojourner were identified as being the responsibility of the entire community, which was to provide for their needs and protect them. What is at stake here is these persons' vulnerability, which is a consequence of their life circumstance. Children are by definition vulnerable and in need of care and protection by adults. When this care and protection are not provided by adults, and when those whose responsibility it is to protect are in fact the source of pain and abuse, then someone else must act to provide for the child. Such is the situation faced by a religious leader to whom it is disclosed that a child may be abused.

The other ethical principle that applies here is that of "justice-making" in response to harm done by one person to another. Christian scripture here is very specific:

"Take heed to yourselves if your brother sins, rebuke him, and if he repents, forgive him" (Luke 17:3, NRSV). The one who harms another must be confronted so that he might seek repentance. Both Hebrew and Christian scriptures are clear that repentance has to do with change: "get yourselves a new heart and a new spirit! . . . so turn and live" (Ezekiel 18:31–32, NRSV). The Greek word used for repentance is *metanoia*, "to have another mind." In this context of repentance, accountability, and justice, forgiveness and reconciliation may be possible. These should be the primary concerns of the religious leader.

FINAL GOALS

As with all forms of family violence, child abuse requires an immediate response and a recognition of a larger context. The goals of any effective response should follow this order:

1. Protect the child from further abuse.
2. Stop the abuser's violence.
3. Heal the victim's brokenness and, if possible, restore the family relationships; if not possible, mourn the loss of that relationship.

Taking these steps in order provides the best possible opportunity for eventual restoration of the family. Until the first two goals are successfully accomplished, the third is unachievable. It is certainly possible to have the victim and offender living in the same place and giving the appearance of being an intact family, but unless the victim is safe and the offender has taken steps to stop the abuse, there is no restoration and no intact family.

In situations of child abuse, these goals can best be accomplished by the early reporting of suspected child abuse to legal authorities. Every state in the United States provides a mechanism at the state level for reporting investigating, and assessing situations where children may be at risk. They also have the professional resources with which to assist victims, abusers, and other family members in addressing the three goals of intervention.

REPORTING: REASONS TO REPORT

1. Facts about child abuse:

Offenders will reoffend unless they get specialized treatment.

Offenders against children minimize, lie, and deny their abusive behavior.

Offenders rarely follow through on their good intentions or genuine remorse without help from the outside.

Treatment of offenders is most effective when it is ordered and monitored by the courts.

The pattern of the abuse must be broken in order to get help to the victim and offender.

Quick forgiveness of the offender is likely to be "cheap grace" and is unlikely to lead to repentance and change. These factors emphasize the need to use an external, authoritative, specialized resource in order to bring change for the family.

2. *Access to specialized resources for treatment:* Unless the ministers are specially trained to provide treatment for victims and abusers of family violence, they alone are not an adequate resource to the family. The pastor's role is critical throughout, but the most important first step is reporting.

3. *Access to a means to protect a child and require accountability from an offender:* The child protective service or law enforcement offices in a community are the only bodies authorized to investigate allegations of abuse, provide physical protection for a child, and restrain the behavior of an adult who is abusive.

4. *Deprivatizing the situation:* Involving the services of a community agency requires that the silence that has supported this chronic situation be broken. It is not simply a private, family matter; it is a community concern. The consequences can no longer be avoided. Again, this offers the best chance to provide help to a hurting family.

5. *Setting a norm:* Involvement of the wider community clearly communicates to all involved that the physical, sexual, or emotional abuse or neglect of a child is intolerable because children are important and it is our collective responsibility to protect them.

6. *Mandatory:* In every state, persons in helping professions are man dated to report the suspicion of child abuse to the authorities. In some states, the religious leader is exempt from this requirement. In every state, any citizen *may* report suspected child abuse and not be liable for an unfounded report if the report is made in good faith. With or without a legal mandate, clergy should consider the weight of an ethical mandate to report.

WHY MINISTERS MAY HESITATE

The ambivalence many ministers feel about reporting child abuse comes at the point when other considerations supersede the fundamental goal of protecting the child. Such things as protecting family privacy or the status of the adults in the family, fears of breaking up the family, or perceptions of the social service providers as punitive or insensitive to the religious beliefs of the family make it difficult for a religious leader to refer or report. Yet once ministers receive a disclosure, they have the authority and responsibility to protect children who cannot protect themselves.

REPORTING: HOW-TO'S

Sometimes the hesitancy to report comes from a lack of understanding of what will happen once a report is made. Every state has a statewide agency responsible for child protection.[1] Generally, a report is made to indicate there is suspicion that a child is being harmed. The religious leader need not have specific evidence and need not attempt to gather evidence or detailed information from the person who discloses. If it sounds as if abuse may have occurred and the child is still at risk, then the child protection agency should be notified. It will investigate the situation and assess the risk to the child. In some communities, it will encourage the alleged abuser to temporarily leave the home. Frequently, when there is no other available option, it will remove the child temporarily from the home. If there is evidence of abuse, it will take the case to the prosecutor, who will then decide whether to file charges. Whether charges are filed or not, the child protection agency will offer counseling to the child victim and nonoffending family members. If the abuser is convicted, the court may mandate counseling as an alternative to prison time. Adults seldom serve time for child abuse convictions.

PROBLEMS AND SUGGESTIONS

Another cause for hesitation in the religious leader is the fear that reporting will be perceived by abusers as turning them in and thus will damage, perhaps irrevocably, the pastoral relationship. Two factors militate against this fear. First, it is seldom the abuser who discloses; it is most likely the child/teenage victim or the nonoffending family member who calls for help. Second, the way in which the report is made significantly shapes the perception of the person who has disclosed.

For example, if a religious leader conveys any ambivalence to someone at the first hint of abuse by saying, "Don't tell me any more or I will have to report this," the context is set for a punitive and secretive situation. The minister is also withholding possible assistance from the person who is seeking help. Further, it is not helpful for the minister to listen to a disclosure, never indicating that a report must be made, then wait until the person leaves to call and report anonymously. This may relieve the conscience, but does not help create a context in which the religious leader can continue to minister as a part of wider intervention.

Instead, it is helpful when hearing a disclosure to indicate that additional help will be needed in order to aid the victim, save the family, help the abuser, and so forth, and that the best resource to begin with is the child protection service. Suggest that the person who has disclosed call the agency with you present, and offer to be with them when the social service provider comes to talk with them. Help the person disclosing to understand that the child protection worker can provide much more in addition to what you can do and reassure the discloser that you will not desert him or her. Then seek to work *with* the child protective service worker to provide for the needs of the members of the family seeking help.

WHAT TO EXPECT WITH DISCLOSURE/REPORTING

Offenders will frequently be the last people you would expect to sexually molest a child. They may well be highly regarded, upstanding citizens who are active in the congregation. Do not allow your impression of these people in public settings to prevent you from entertaining the possibility that they may have molested a child.

Initially, the offender will usually deny all responsibility and will seek to discredit the victim's story by attacking its credibility: "She lies about everything, but this is the most ridiculous one she's told yet." It is always tempting to believe the adult's denial because our society has never taken children's words very seriously.

Very rarely do victims falsely report an offense. If they have summoned the courage to tell someone about their situation, they almost always have been harmed by someone. Victims may also quickly recant their story because they feel extreme pressure from family members and maybe even the offender to do so. Their recantation does not mean the abuse did not occur or that this person is now safe. Nonoffending family members (usually mothers) initially may not believe their child, but instead feel pressure to support the offender against the child. The mother may also be a victim of spouse abuse.

When a report is made to the legal authorities, chaos usually erupts. The whole family is in crisis. It may take several weeks for this very complex situation to be sorted out. The results of disclosure and reporting may not be a final resolution to the incestuous abuse situation in a family, but some attention to this matter is better than none.

SPECIAL CONSIDERATIONS

Confessions and Confidentiality

Many people in pastoral roles perceive a contradiction between their obligation to preserve confidentiality of communication with a congregant and their obligation to report the suspicion of child abuse. They see this contradiction as a conflict of ethical demands. Part of the perceived conflict arises from the interpretation of confidentiality and its purpose, particularly as it rests within the responsibility of the religious professional. The context for an analysis of these ethical demands is the understanding of confidentiality that comes to the religious professional from multiple sources.

The purpose of confidentiality has been to provide a safe place for a congregant or client to share concerns, questions, or burdens without fear of disclosure. It provides a context of respect and trust, within which help can hopefully be provided for an individual. It has meant that some people have come forward seeking help who might not otherwise have done so out of fear of punishment or embarrassment. Confidentiality has traditionally been the ethical responsibility of the professional within a professional relationship and is generally assumed to be operative even if a specific request has not been made by the congregant or client.

For the minister, unlike the secular helping professional, confidentiality rests in the context of spiritual issues and expectations. In Christian denominations, the expectations of confidentiality lie most specifically within the experience of confession. The responsibility of the pastor or priest ranges from a strict understanding to a more flexible one-from the letter to the spirit of the law. For example, for Anglican and Roman Catholic priests, the confessional occasion with a penitent person is sacramental; whatever information is revealed is held in confidence by the seal of confession, with no exceptions.[2] The United Methodist *Book of Discipline* does not view confession as sacramental but states, "Ministers . . . are charged to maintain all confidences inviolate, including confessional confidences."[3] The Lutheran Church in America protect the confidence of the parishioner and allows for the discretion of the pastor: "no minister . . . shall divulge any confidential disclosure given to him in the course of his care of souls or otherwise in his professional capacity, except with the express permission of the person who has confided in him or in order to prevent a crime."[4] Even within Christian denominations, there is a range of interpretations of the expectations of confidentiality which are not necessarily limited to the confessional occasion.

What Are Confidentiality and Secrecy?

It may be useful to distinguish between confidentiality and secrecy. Secrecy is the absolute promise never under any circumstance to share any information that comes to a member of the clergy; this is the essence of sacramental confession. But a commitment to secrecy may also support maintaining the secret of child abuse, which probably means that the abuse will continue. Confidentiality means to hold information in trust and to share it with others only in the interest of the person involved, with their permission, in order to seek consultation with another professional. Information may also be shared without violating confidentiality in order to protect others from harm. Confidentiality is intended as a means to help an individual get help for a problem and prevent further harm to herself or others. Confidentiality is not intended to protect abusers from being held account able for their actions or to keep them from getting the help they need. Shield ing them from the consequence of their behavior will likely further endanger their victims and will deny them the repentance they need.

In addition, confidentiality is not intended to protect professionals; it is for those whom they serve. It should not be used as a shield to protect incompetent or negligent colleagues or to protect them from professional obligations. Thus, confidentiality may be invoked for all the wrong reasons and not truly in the interest of a particular congregant or of society. This was never the intent of this special provision of pastoral communication.

Disclosure within Different Faiths

When a disclosure is made by an offender in a confessional setting, the religious leader has the opportunity to respond within the parameters of a particular faith's tradition while keeping in mind the overriding priority of protecting the child victim. For example, a Roman Catholic priest can hear the confession of a child abuser, prescribe penance to report himself to the child protection service, and withhold absolution until the penance is accomplished. Confession to a priest does not carry with it the priest's obligation to absolve in the absence of penitent acts. Confession opens the opportunity for the penitent persons to repent and to make right the harm they have done to others. Likewise, for a Protestant in a non-sacramental confessional situation, directives may be given and actions prescribed that include the abuser reporting himself to child protection services. If it is clear that the penitent will not follow the directive of the religious leader and self-report, then some Protestant ministers have the option and the obligation to report directly. The vulnerability of the child and the significant likelihood that the abuse will continue supersede an obligation to maintain in confidence the confession of the penitent.

Cooperation: Working with Secular Service Providers

In addition to a long-standing breach between religious and secular professionals concerned with mental health issues, some substantive concerns have often prevented ministers from working effectively with social service providers or therapists. All these concerns come to the fore when the issue of reporting child abuse is raised: separation of church and state, involvement of the criminal justice system, disregard for a family's religious beliefs, and breaking up families. While the state should not interfere with the practice of ministry, it does have the lawful responsibility of protecting children from harm. The church should see this as a common agenda and work with those designated to carry out this mandate. Even with its multitude of shortcomings (not the least of which are sexism and racism), the criminal justice system can provide a mechanism to enforce accountability for offenders and should not be avoided to protect offenders from embarrassment or the serious consequences of their abuse. A family's religious beliefs deserve respect. But any effort by family members to use religious beliefs to justify abuse of a child or deflect intervention intended to stop abuse should be challenged by both religious and secular professionals. Finally, outside intervention to protect a child does not break up the family. The abuse which preceded the intervention broke up the family and endangered its members. Temporary separation of family members may well be the only possible means of healing and restoration, and should be used when appropriate.

Cooperation between religious and secular professionals expands the resources available to a family experiencing abuse. The special skills each can bring are much needed by family members. Religious leaders can concentrate on their pastoral responsibilities in concert with the social service provider, who can guide the intervention and treatment.

CONCLUSION

Situations of suspected child abuse are seldom simple and straightforward. Religious leaders should be guided by a commitment to the overriding priority of protection of children and by a clear sense of the limits of their own resources. The mechanism of reporting child abuse and the resources that follow from it are invaluable tools for the minister. Clarity of purpose will direct an ethical mandate to use every available means to stop the abuse of a child.

Notes

1. Religious leaders should familiarize themselves with the child protective services office in their community. Some child protection programs do only investigation of possible abuse; others do both investigation and treatment. Ask about the specifics of the agency staff's approach to reports and the possible options available to them. Approach them as a professional ally and resource. Invite them to a discussion with local ministerial groups.

2. See Seward Reese, "Confidential Communications to Clergy," *Ohio State Law Journal,* 24 (1963), 55.

3. *The Book of Discipline of the United Methodist Church* (Nashville, Tenn.: United Methodist Publishing House, 1980), 220, paragraph 440.4.

4. *The Minutes of the United Lutheran Church in America,* 22nd Biennial Convention, 1960, as quoted in Reese, "Confidential Communications," 69.

Notes

FOREWORD

1. Sue Woodman, "How Teen Pregnancy Has Become a Political Football," *Ms.*, Jan./Feb. 1995. "Some 74 percent of women who had intercourse before age 14 and 60 percent of those who had sex before age 15 report having had sex involuntarily" (Sex and America's Teenagers, The Alan Guttmacher Institute, 1994). Ordinarily we call this rape. The older a young woman gets, the less likely she is to have experienced "involuntary sex."

2. June Larkin and Katherine Popaleni, "Heterosexual Courtship Violence and Sexual Harassment: The Private and Public Control of Young Women," *Feminism and Psychology,* 4, no. 2 (1994), 218.

3. Ibid.

4. Rachael Horsfield, "Why Blondes Don't Have More Fun," *The Age,* 1 May 1991, 16.

5. For excellent curricula, see *Created in God's Image: A Human Sexuality Program for Ministry and Mission* and *Affirming Persons—Saving Lives: AIDS Awareness and Prevention Education,* both from the United Church of Christ. See also Marie Fortune, *Love Does No Harm: Sexual Ethics for the Rest of Us* (New York: Continuum, 1995).

1. GOD'S GIFT OF SEXUALITY

1. From the Introduction to *Sexuality and the Sacred: Sources for Theological Reflection,* ed. James B. Nelson and Sandra P. Longfellow (Louisville: Westminster John Knox, 1994), xiv.

2. The discussion of continuums is taken from Marie M. Fortune, *Sexual Violence: The Unmentionable Sin* (New York: Pilgrim Press, 1983), 30–38. In preparation for this discussion, it might be helpful to read this section.

3. Cited from Ellen Bass and Laura Davis, *The Courage to Heal* (New York: Harper and Row, 1988).

2. THE POWERFUL AND THE VULNERABLE: SEXUAL HARASSMENT

1. Much of the information in this session is taken from *Clergy Misconduct: Sexual Abuse in the Ministerial Relationship—Trainer's Manual* (Seattle: Center for the Prevention of Sexual and Domestic Violence, 1992), IV–62 to IV–66.

3. THE GOOD, THE BAD, AND THE CONFUSING

1. This information is found in "The Child Sexual Abuse Prevention Guidebook," Sexual Assault Services, Hennepin County Attorney's Office, Minneapolis, Minn., 1979. The Touch Continuum has been further developed through dance and theater presentations to groups of children. Cordelia Anderson can be contacted through the Illusion Theatre, 528 Hennepin Ave. #704, Minneapolis, MN 55403, (612) 339-4944.

2. It is important to emphasize that we are not saying that intentions don't matter. The problem is that the other person does not know what the intention is. Thus,

a touch that was given with good intentions may not be received as such. Because of this, it is important to highlight the *received experience* as the criterion for determining the value of the touch.

3. Information for this section was also drawn from Kathryn Goering Reid, *Preventing Child Sexual Abuse: Ages 5–8* (Cleveland: United Church Press, 1994), 57–60, and *Clergy Misconduct: Sexual Abuse in the Ministerial Relationship—Trainer's Manual* (Seattle: Center for the Prevention of Sexual and Domestic Violence, 1992), III–39 to III–41.

4. Ellen Bass and Laura Davis, *The Courage to Heal: A Guide for Women Survivors of Child Sexual Abuse,* 3d ed. (New York: Harper Perennial, 1994). In this quotation, the authors are citing information from *Conspiracy of Silence* by Sandra Butler, *The Best Kept Secret* by Florence Rush, *Sexually Victimized Children* and *Child Sexual Abuse* by David Finkelhor, and *The Secret Trauma* by Diana E. H. Russell.

4. THE DANGER OF THE DREAMWORLDS

1. It is important to note that this discussion refers to the larger culture in the United States. Although other countries have cultures that discriminate, the particular dynamics to which we are referring are in the United States. Also, there are different dynamics within different subcultures in this country. Some may respect women more than others, some may value gays and lesbians, etc. However, this discussion focuses on society at large.

5. THIS IS VIOLENCE, NOT LOVE

1. D. Sugarman and G. Hotaling, "Dating Violence: A Review of Contextual and Risk Factors," *Dating Violence: Young Women in Danger,* ed. B. Levy (Seattle: Seal Press, 1991).

2. S. Ageton, *Sexual Assault Among Adolescents* (Lexington, Mass.: D. C. Heath, 1983); Barrie Levy, *In Love and in Danger: A Teen's Guide to Breaking Free of Abusive Relationships* (Seattle: Seal Press, 1993), 28.

3. Marie M. Fortune, *Sexual Violence: The Unmentionable Sin* (New York: The Pilgrim Press, 1998), 7.

4. Robin Warshaw, *I Never Called It Rape: The Ms. Report on Recognizing, Fighting, and Surviving Date and Acquaintance Rape* (New York: Harper and Row, 1988), 12.

5. Ibid., 83–97.

6. Ibid, 92.

7. The continuum draws on material from Scott Allen Johnson, *Man to Man: When Your Partner Says No—Pressured Sex and Date Rape* (Orwell, Vt.: Safer Society Press, 1992), 24–26, and June Larkin and Katherine Popaleni, "Heterosexual Courtship Violence and Sexual Harassment: The Private and Public Control of Young Women," *Feminism and Psychology* 4, no. 2 (May 1994).

8. "Rating" is a popular practice with many teenagers, primarily boys. As a young woman walks down the school hall, each boy will put up a card or fingers showing what "score" he would give her. Most often, the rating a boy gives a girl is based on popularity and looks.

6. THIS IS ABOUT LOVE

1. From the Introduction to *Sexuality and the Sacred: Sources for Theological Reflection,* ed. James B. Nelson and Sandra P. Longfellow (Louisville: Westminster John Knox, 1994), xiv.

2. This concept is drawn from Scott Allen Johnson, *Man-to-Man: When Your Partner Says No—Pressured Sex and Date Rape* (Orwell, Vt.: Safer Society Press, 1992), 7.

Resources

BOOKS AND ARTICLES

Abuse Prevention

Mary Nelson, *Educator's Guide to Preventing Child Sexual Abuse* (Santa Cruz, Calif.: Network, 1986).

Elizabeth Powell, *Talking Back to Sexual Pressure: What to Say to Resist Pressure* (Minneapolis: CompCare, 1991).

Lois Loontjens, *Talking to Children/Talking to Parents About Sexual Assault* (Santa Cruz, Calif.: Network, 1984).

Cultural Issues

June Larkin and Katherine Popaleni, "Heterosexual Courtship Violence and Sexual Harassment: The Private and Public Control of Young Women," *Feminism and Psychology* 4, no. 2 (May 1994).

Dating Violence

Barrie Levy, *Dating Violence: Young Women in Danger* (Seattle: Seal Press, 1991).

Barrie Levy, *In Love and In Danger: A Teen's Guide to Breaking Free of Abusive Relationships* (Seattle: Seal Press, 1993).

Ethical/Theological Issues

Marie M. Fortune, *Love Does No Harm: Sexual Ethics for the Rest of Us* (New York: Continuum, 1995).

Marie M. Fortune, *Sexual Violence: The Unmentionable Sin* (New York: The Pilgrim Press, 1983).

James B. Nelson and Sandra P. Longfellow, eds., *Sexuality and the Sacred: Sources for Theological Reflection* (Louisville: Westminster John Knox, 1994).

Pedagogical Issues

Parker Palmer, *To Know As We Are Known: Education as a Spiritual Journey* (San Francisco: Harper San Francisco, 1993).

Resources Especially for Men and Boys

Scott Allen Johnson, *Man-to-Man: When Your Partner Says No—Pressured Sex and Date Rape* (Orwell, Vt.: Safer Society Press/New York State Council of Churches, 1992).

Paul Kivel, *Men's Work: How to Stop the Violence That Tears Our Lives Apart* (Center City, Minn.: Hazelden Educational Materials, 1992).

Paul Kivel, *Men's Work (Facilitator's Guide): A Complete Counseling Plan for Breaking the Cycle of Male Violence* (Center City, Minn.: Hazelden Educational Materials, 1993).

John Stoltenberg, *Refusing to Be a Man* (New York: Penguin/Meridian, 1993).

Sexual Abuse Survivors

Am I the Only One?: A Book of Information for Children Who Have Been Sexually Abused (Aberdeen, Oh.: American Legion Post 59, 1987).

Ellen Bass and Laura Davis, *The Courage to Heal: A Guide for Women Survivors of Child Sexual Abuse* (New York: HarperCollins, 1992).

Laura Davis, *The Courage to Heal Workbook for Women and Men Survivors of Child Sexual Abuse* (New York: Harper and Row, 1990).

Cynthia L. Mather, *How Long Does It Hurt? A Guide to Recovering from Incest and Sexual Abuse for Teenagers, Their Friends, and Their Families* (San Francisco: Jossey-Bass, 1994).

Jane A. W. Satullo, *It Happens to Boys Too . . .* (Pittsfield, Mass.: Rape Crisis Center of the Berkshires, 1989).

Barbara Bean and Shari Bennett, *The Me Nobody Knows: A Guide for Teen Survivors* (New York: Lexington Books, Macmillan, 1993).

Mike Lew, *Victims No Longer: Men Recovering from Incest and Other Sexual Child Abuse* (New York: HarperCollins, 1990).

Sexual Harassment

June Larkin, *Sexual Harassment: High School Girls Speak Out* (Toronto: Second Story Press, 1994).

VIDEOS

Used in the Curriculum

Dreamworlds II. 55 minutes. Produced by Media Education Foundation. This video is available for rental from the Washington Coalition of Sexual Assault Programs, 110 E. 5th Ave., Suite 214, Olympia, WA 98501 (360) 754-7583. The rental fee is $8. (Used in Session 4.)

Out of Bounds: Sexual Harassment. 18 minutes. Produced by Coronet/MTI Film and Video. This video is available for rental from the Washington Coalition of Sexual Assault Programs, 110 E. 5th Ave., Suite 214, Olympia, WA 98501 (360) 754-7583. The rental fee is $8. (Used in Session 2.)

Scoring: Date Rape. 20 minutes. Produced by Coronet/MTI Film and Video. This video is available for rental from the Washington Coalition of Sexual Assault Programs, 110 E. 5th Ave., Suite 214, Olympia, WA 98501 (360) 754-7583. The rental fee is $8. (Used in Session 5).

Recommended for Preparation

Hear Their Cries: Religious Responses to Child Abuse. 48 minutes. Produced by the Center for the Prevention of Sexual and Domestic Violence.

Bless Our Children: Preventing Sexual Abuse. 40 minutes. Produced by the Center for the Prevention of Sexual and Domestic Violence.

Both of these videos are excellent tools aimed at church audiences. They highlight and examine the primary issues involved with child abuse and outline how churches and synagogues can respond. *Hear Their Cries* provides a good overview of the issue and illustrates one pastor's effective response to a teenager's disclosure of abuse. *Bless Our Children* is a case study of the process one congregation went through in order to implement a child sexual abuse prevention curriculum in its Sunday school program. It contains classroom scenes illustrating how to talk with both young children and teenagers about abuse prevention. It also shows one teacher hearing the disclosure of abuse by one of her students.

Both videos are available for rental and/or purchase from the Center for the Prevention of Sexual and Domestic Violence, 936 N. 34th Street, Suite 200, Seattle, WA 98103, (206) 634-1903.

A third video is forthcoming from the Center for the Prevention of Sexual and Domestic Violence. It will focus specifically on teenagers and abuse. For more information, contact the Center at (206) 634-1903.

Other Videos

I Know You Said No but I Thought You Meant Yes. Produced by Cornell University. For rental or purchase, call (607) 255-2091. The *New England College Sexual Assault Network Directory* has this to say about this video: "Acquaintance rape dynamics for high school students. Good trigger sequences." They also give it a 4 out of 5 on their rating scale.

Still Killing Us Softly. Produced by Documentary Films, Cambridge, Mass. The *New England College Sexual Assault Network Directory* has this to say about this video: "Excellent ideas presented about how the media perpetuates a culture that accepts/promotes sexual violence and objectification of women."